**New Directions for
Teaching and Learning**

Catherine M. Wehlburg
EDITOR-IN-CHIEF

Looking and Learning: Visual Literacy across the Disciplines

Deandra Little
Peter Felten
Chad Berry

EDITORS

Number 141 • Spring 2015
Jossey-Bass
San Francisco

LOOKING AND LEARNING: VISUAL LITERACY ACROSS THE DISCIPLINES
Deandra Little, Peter Felten, Chad Berry (eds.)
New Directions for Teaching and Learning, no. 141
Catherine M. Wehlburg, Editor-in-Chief

Microfilm copies of issues and articles are available in 16 mm and 35 mm, as well as microfiche in 105 mm, through University Microfilms, Inc., 300 North Zeeb Road, Ann Arbor, MI 48106-1346.

NEW DIRECTIONS FOR TEACHING AND LEARNING (ISSN 0271-0633, electronic ISSN 1536-0768) is part of The Jossey-Bass Higher and Adult Education Series and is published quarterly by Wiley Subscription Services, Inc., A Wiley Company, at Jossey-Bass, One Montgomery Street, Suite 1200, San Francisco, CA 94104-4594. POSTMASTER: Send address changes to New Directions for Teaching and Learning, Jossey-Bass, One Montgomery Street, Suite 1200, San Francisco, CA 94104-4594.

New Directions for Teaching and Learning is indexed in CIJE: Current Index to Journals in Education (ERIC), Contents Pages in Education (T&F), Educational Research Abstracts Online (T&F), ERIC Database (Education Resources Information Center), Higher Education Abstracts (Claremont Graduate University), and SCOPUS (Elsevier).

INDIVIDUAL SUBSCRIPTION RATE (in USD): $89 per year US/Can/Mex, $113 rest of world; institutional subscription rate: $335 US, $375 Can/Mex, $409 rest of world. Single copy rate: $29. Electronic only–all regions: $89 individual, $335 institutional; Print & Electronic–US: $98 individual, $402 institutional; Print & Electronic–Can/Mex: $98 individual, $442 institutional; Print & Electronic–rest of world: $122 individual, $476 institutional.

Cover design: Wiley
Cover Images: © Lava 4 images | Shutterstock

EDITORIAL CORRESPONDENCE should be sent to the editor-in-chief, Catherine M. Wehlburg, c.wehlburg@tcu.edu.

www.josseybass.com

CONTENTS

FROM THE SERIES EDITOR

About This Publication

Since 1980, *New Directions for Teaching and Learning* (NDTL) has brought a unique blend of theory, research, and practice to leaders in postsecondary education. NDTL sourcebooks strive not only for solid substance but also for timeliness, compactness, and accessibility.

The series has four goals: to inform readers about current and future directions in teaching and learning in postsecondary education, to illuminate the context that shapes these new directions, to illustrate these new direction through examples from real settings, and to propose ways in which these new directions can be incorporated into still other settings.

This publication reflects the view that teaching deserves respect as a high form of scholarship. We believe that significant scholarship is conducted not only by researchers who report results of empirical investigations but also by practitioners who share disciplinary reflections about teaching. Contributors to NDTL approach questions of teaching and learning as seriously as they approach substantive questions in their own disciplines, and they deal not only with pedagogical issues but also with the intellectual and social context in which these issues arise. Authors deal on the one hand with theory and research and on the other with practice, and they translate from research and theory to practice and back again.

About This Volume

Visual images are memorable. Much of the research in the area of memory and lifelong learning seems to support the rationale that we learn quickly and deeply through images. This volume is focused on teaching and learning with visuals and provides innovative examples of teaching with images in both disciplinary and interdisciplinary contexts. The authors within this volume connect visual literacy theory directly to classroom practices and student learning. The chapter authors describe and also analyze their use of innovative techniques that help students make meaning of images within the specific context that they were created and viewed. I am very pleased to present to you, the reader, this important volume that truly integrates theory with practice.

Catherine M. Wehlburg
Editor-in-Chief

EDITORS' NOTES

We live in a visual world. Historians (including two of the three editors of this volume) tend to be deeply skeptical of "never-before" statements, but, in this case, *never before* seems an apt description of the way that technology has brought digital images to the lives of sighted people. Each day, each hour, each minute, connected people are able to retrieve, manipulate, and share images through computer or mobile devices with a worldwide audience; such a phenomenon only builds on earlier media developments in the twentieth century (Sturken and Cartwright 2001). Full-time news cycles further saturate our lives with the latest tweeted image or YouTube video; viewers rarely have the time to ponder the meanings before the next images arrive. Images sometimes appear to be both the means and the message in our lives. Cultural critic W. J. T. Mitchell presciently wrote (way back) in 1994 that the "problem of the twenty-first century is the problem of the image" (2). Today, such a statement seems almost banal given the inundation of images in our lives.

The sheer volume of images might lead some to dismiss the significance of this visual flood. Some skeptics may write it off as lowbrow detritus of a shallow media age, while others might assume that today's university students are "visual natives" who have grown up in an environment that prepares them to be more visually sophisticated than those of us who came of age in the predigital era (see Prensky 2001). Both of those views are flawed.

Learning to look, it turns out, is more complicated than it seems. The mechanics of vision are so apparently familiar as to be misleading. Vision is the primary way sighted individuals gather information about the world. More than a third of the human brain is devoted to the process of seeing, and much of this process is automatic, efficient, and largely effortless. Yet vision is not a passive process. The seemingly simple act of seeing is an "active construction" (Hoffman 1989, xii) that encompasses both the physical interaction of light with our visual systems and the rational, emotional, and social ways we learn to make meaning from experiences and memories. As photographer and critic Susan Sontag (1977, 2003) reminds us, seeing can be deceiving; we do not all see the same thing even when we are looking at the very same image. William James (1890/2007) made this point well more than a century ago: "Whilst part of what we perceive comes through our senses from the object before us, another part (and it may be the larger part) always comes out of our own mind" (2:103).

While James's focus is psychology and Sontag's is photographs, faculty in higher education classrooms often encounter similar complexity. For instance, Place, Hillyard, and Thomas (2008) vividly describe a moment in a particular class when they realized that an activity using video clips was not succeeding in the way they had intended. Their students interpreted the videos far differently from the ways the authors had initially thought were "obvious," reminding them that "[v]isual modes are particularly seductive" because "codes and conventions appear over time as natural, real and transparent to viewers" (77). As they point out, often we assume our students can look at an image and see just what (and as) we do. However, experts in any field have learned how to look; they know what to look for and what to screen out. Novices in the field, on the other hand, may be confused by too much or irrelevant information present in the perceptual field. This is not surprising, of course. The same expert–novice gap is apparent in all facets of teaching a discipline; students need to learn to conduct an experiment, to read a poem, and to analyze a data set. The same is true for visual capacities. Looking carefully, particularly through a disciplinary lens, is a complex process that must be learned.

The art historian James Elkins connects this complexity and the ubiquity of visuals to argue, flatly, that "Images are central to our lives ... it is time they are central in our universities" (Elkins 2007, 8). As we noted in an article in *Liberal Education*, however, college and university classrooms rarely acknowledge, let alone teach, students to make disciplinary or other meaning with visual sources (Little, Felten, and Berry 2010). Exceptions exist, and some disciplines excel at cultivating visual capacities in students, but too few students are afforded the opportunity to develop their visual skills. Indeed, Carmen Luke points to the ways visual meaning is often intentionally minimized in university classrooms, where interpreting written texts takes priority, making most college classes the only time students are *not* "blending, mixing, and matching knowledge drawn from diverse textual sources and communications media" to understand the world and express themselves (Luke 2003, 398). Just as listening to a playlist on an iPod does not teach a person to listen critically to music, let alone to create it, using the various platforms in which visuals predominate—from the Internet to Instagram—does not necessarily instruct users or viewers in analysis or construction (Felten 2008). When researchers note that many students are not learning to read and write with texts, an uproar ensues about students being "academically adrift" (Arum and Roksa 2010). And, many higher institutions have sophisticated programs and curricular structures to develop progressively their students as writers, a development that certainly is an essential part of higher education. In today's world, however, visual skills are no different; students bring some capacities with them to campus, but even the strongest students should be challenged and supported to further hone their abilities to make meaning with and from visuals.

To do that, faculty and colleges will need to cultivate visual literacy across the curriculum. The term visual literacy was coined in the 1960s by John Debes, who cofounded the International Visual Literacy Association, and he offered an initial attempt at defining the concept: "a group of vision-competencies a human being can develop by seeing and at the same time having and integrating other sensory experiences" (Fransecky and Debes 1972, 7).

To make the term more useful to nonexperts, Barbara Seels emphasized visual learning, visual thinking, and visual communication as the most basic and important components of visual literacy (Seels 1994). More recently, James Elkins simultaneously clarified and complicated these definitions, explaining that visual literacy involves "understanding how people perceive objects, interpret what they see, and what they learn from them" (Elkins 2007, 2). More simply, Felten claimed that visual literacy "involves the ability to understand, produce, and use culturally significant images, objects, and visible actions" (Felten 2008, 60).

A strength and challenge of visual literacy as a mode of inquiry is its expansive nature. Many different thinkers approach it from a virtually endless array of perspectives: the fine arts and design, certainly, but also philosophical, conceptual, communicative, pedagogical, and neuroscientific to name but a few (Avgerinou and Pettersson 2011). To help identify broad but specific, cross-disciplinary visual literacy skills that students should master in college, in 2011, the Association of College and Research Libraries (ACRL) published "Visual Literacy Competency Standards for Higher Education." The ACRL defined visual literacy as "a set of abilities that enables an individual to effectively find, interpret, evaluate, use, and create images and visual media" (ACRL 2011, para. 2). By emphasizing observable performance standards linked to that definition, the ACRL aimed to establish a framework that will help institutions and individuals develop visual literacy in college students. In this approach, a visually literate student

1. determines the nature and extent of the visual materials needed;
2. finds and accesses needed images and visual media effectively and efficiently;
3. interprets and analyzes the meanings of images and visual media;
4. evaluates images and their sources;
5. uses images and visual media effectively;
6. designs and creates meaningful images and visual media; and

7. understands many of the ethical, legal, social, and economic issues surrounding the creation and use of images and visual media, and accesses and uses visual materials ethically.

These interdisciplinary standards are particularly helpful because they illustrate that serious efforts to cultivate visual literacy across the curriculum must involve not only faculty but also librarians, learning technologists, faculty developers, and others.

Developing visual literacy is not only an important end in itself. This work will also yield important outcomes linked to two central pillars of higher education:

1. *Learning within a discipline.* Cultivating visual literacy moves students toward the heart of many disciplines. This may be obvious in fields such as art history, but it is no less true, for instance, in STEM (science, technology, engineering, and mathematics) fields that make meaning with visual representations of data, often voluminous amounts of data. One of the purposes of this volume is to provide ideas about and applications of visual literacy within and across disciplines.

2. *Learning skills associated with liberal education,* including both how to interpret and create images and broader learning outcomes such as critical thinking, analytical writing, and self-expression. These essential skills are cultivated regularly in a few disciplines and in some general education programs, but they are no less relevant or important in any field a student may choose to study. Sociology, political science, and business students, for instance, must develop sophisticated skills to read and write with the kinds of images that shape our cultural, political, and economic lives.

By looking and learning in both discipline-specific and cross-disciplinary ways, students develop capacities to make meaning in the world, which is a visual environment. After all, given the barrage of images bombarding sighted individuals today, none of these images is necessarily bound within one particular discipline, suggesting that richer meaning is possible through both deeper and broader connections.

This volume's chapters sit at intersections of these visual literacy outcomes. Each chapter explores how visual pedagogies or tools help students develop disciplinary knowledge and skills. Each also offers practical advice and inspiration for educators across the disciplines and in diverse roles; indeed, each contributor aims to entice readers, regardless of discipline, to think in new ways about visuals in the classroom and the curriculum.

Astronomy professor Anthony Crider (Chapter 1) describes classroom activities and assignments that help students learn to analyze and produce a range of visuals fundamental to astronomical and more broadly scientific thinking.

NEW DIRECTIONS FOR TEACHING AND LEARNING • DOI: 10.1002/tl

Chemist Michael S. Palmer (Chapter 2) highlights a variety of ways visuals engage students and deepen learning in an interdisciplinary first-year course, focusing specifically on strategies that help students move from quick assumptions to more careful analysis.

Sociologist and documentarian Katherine Hyde (Chapter 3) describes assignments that prompt students to cultivate "sociological mindfulness" in which students learn disciplinary frameworks for inquiry into the world around them while they strengthen their observation and communication skills through photography.

Cedar Riener (Chapter 4), a professor of cognitive psychology, explains how he uses a variety of optical illusions to help students not only understand the complexity of visual perception but also begin questioning broadly held assumptions about how they "see" the world. Riener offers suggestions for how instructors in a range of fields might include these illusions to frame conversations about the nature of disciplinary knowledge making.

Historian Steven S. Volk (Chapter 5) explores the complexity of teaching students how to use images as historical sources. In the process, he addresses a series of issues that span across disciplines, including ways to help students learn to focus their attention as well as working with students who have limited sight in image-rich courses.

French professor Alison J. Murray Levine (Chapter 6) blends theory and practice in an upper-level French film class to help deepen and enrich students' abilities to engage with visual material, strengthening their observational and analytical skills in the process.

Visual communications professor Phillip Motley (Chapter 7) considers the ways visual critique can help students learn to interpret, evaluate, and provide thoughtful feedback on visual images in a variety of contexts.

In conclusion (Chapter 8), Deandra Little offers general strategies for integrating visuals into any higher education classroom.

Given the pace of change related to technology, accessibility, and connectability, images have not yet plateaued in our culture, either in terms of sheer magnitude or cultural significance. The future is visual. Higher education must prepare our students for the practical, professional, and aesthetic challenges of being consumers and producers of visual meaning. This volume seeks to reveal visions of possibility with visual pedagogies in order to do just that—to deepen our students' sophistication with images across a variety of higher educational disciplines and courses to better prepare them now, and later, to learn to look and to look to learn.

Deandra Little
Peter Felten
Chad Berry
Editors

References

Arum, R., and J. Roksa. 2010. *Academically Adrift: Limited Learning on College Campuses*. Chicago, IL: University of Chicago Press.

Association of College and Research Libraries (ACRL). 2011. "Visual Literacy Competency Standards for Higher Education." http://www.ala.org/acrl/standards/visualliteracy.

Avgerinou, M. D., and R. Pettersson. 2011. "Toward a Cohesive Theory of Visual Literacy." *Journal of Visual Literacy* 30: 1–19.

Elkins, J., ed. 2007. *Visual Literacy*. New York, NY: Routledge.

Felten, P. 2008. "Visual Literacy." *Change* November/December: 60–63.

Fransecky, R. B., and J. L. Debes. 1972. *Visual Literacy: A Way to Learn—A Way to Teach*. Washington, DC: Association for Educational Communications and Technology.

Hoffman, D. 1989. *Visual Intelligence: How We Create What We See*. New York, NY: Norton.

James, W. 1890/2007. *The Principles of Psychology*, vol. 1. New York: Cosimo.

Little, D., P. Felten, and C. Berry. 2010. "Liberal Education in a Visual World." *Liberal Education* 96: 44–49.

Luke, C. 2003. "Pedagogy, Connectivity, Multimodality, and Interdisciplinarity." *Reading Research Quarterly* 38 (July–September): 397–403.

Mitchell, W. J. T. 1994. *Picture Theory: Essays on Verbal and Visual Representation*. Chicago, IL: University of Chicago Press.

Place, N., C. Hillyard, and E. Thomas. 2008. "Students and Teachers Learning to See, Part II: Using Visual Images in the College Classroom to Enhance the Social Context for Learning." *College Teaching* 56: 74–77.

Prensky, M. 2001. "Digital Natives, Digital Immigrants." *On the Horizon* 9: 1–6.

Seels, B. A. 1994. "Visual Literacy: The Definition Problem." In *Visual Literacy: A Spectrum of Visual Learning*, edited by D. M. Moore and F. M. Dwyer, 97–112. Englewood Cliffs, NJ: Educational Technology Publications.

Sontag, S. 1977. *On Photography*. London, UK: Picador.

Sontag, S. 2003. *Regarding the Pain of Others*. London, UK: Picador.

Sturken, M., and L. Cartwright. 2001. *Practices of Looking: An Introduction to Visual Culture*. New York, NY: Oxford University Press.

DEANDRA LITTLE *directs the Center for the Advancement of Teaching and Learning and is an associate professor of English at Elon University.*

PETER FELTEN *is assistant provost, executive director of the Center for Engaged Learning, and professor of history at Elon University.*

CHAD BERRY *is the academic vice president and dean of the faculty, Goode Professor of Appalachian Studies, and professor of history at Berea College.*

1

Astronomy classes that teach students to read and write images, diagrams, and plots offer an ideal venue to teach visual literacy.

Teaching Visual Literacy in the Astronomy Classroom

Anthony Crider

While attending a conference years ago, I asked a colleague to show a video to my class. "Conspiracy Theory: Did We Land on the Moon?" was a misleading documentary-style show that detailed how the Apollo missions to the Moon had been faked. The show, produced in 2001 by FOX Broadcasting Company and hosted by *X-Files* actor Mitch Pileggi, suggested that NASA had perpetrated a hoax on the world: the Moon landings never happened. After the original broadcast, astronomer Phil Plait, in his *Bad Astronomy* blog, outlined the lines of "evidence" from the show and the fallacy in each. For me, the show seemed like a useful learning experience: (1) students would watch (and possibly believe) the video while I was gone at the conference, (2) we would read the blog after I returned, and (3) we would have a good laugh over how silly the hoax believers are. That didn't happen.

The video was very successful in making students question the lunar landings. Clicker quizzes showed that while 10 percent of my students doubted the Moon landing before seeing the video, 50 percent of them became doubters after seeing the video. Worse yet, reading the science blog didn't reverse the damage. The visuals and simplistic (but incorrect) arguments in the FOX video were (unfortunately) very effective; the written scientific explanations were not. I struggled for years to locate visuals or arguments that would reverse the effect of seeing that video and convince students that Neil Armstrong did indeed walk on the Moon! This experiment ultimately led me to change the primary goal of my entire astronomy course. Rather than trying to teach students as much astronomy content as possible in a single semester, I would instead use astronomy to teach them how to stay afloat in the stream of visual images in which they will be swimming for the rest of their lives.

New Directions for Teaching and Learning, no. 141, Spring 2015 © 2015 Wiley Periodicals, Inc.
Published online in Wiley Online Library (wileyonlinelibrary.com) • DOI: 10.1002/tl.20118

Visual Literacy in Higher Education

Students in the twenty-first century are bombarded with visuals crafted to entertain, to inform, and to advertise. Born into a world with three screens (the cinema, the television, and the computer), the advent of cheap LCDs has given them a fourth screen (smartphones, tablets, wearable devices) and more recently a fifth: out-of-home digital signs (for example, restaurant menus showing animated food; Kelsen 2010).

Unfortunately, so far, higher education has largely ignored the rising pervasiveness of a new visual culture. As Little, Felten, and Berry (2010) noted, "visual literacy continues to be marginalized in the national discourse, particularly liberal education" (44). The Association of American Colleges and Universities (AAC&U) alluded to visual communication in 2002 but then eliminated the topic in their 2005 report, *Liberal Education Outcomes*. One of the few academic groups promoting visual literacy is the Association of Colleges and Research Libraries (ACRL), which developed a set of competency standards defining what it means to be a visually literate person (Hattwig et al. 2011). These standards (rewritten slightly so as not to confuse their use of the word "images" with my own in this chapter) require that a visually literate student or instructor

1. determine the nature and extent of the visuals needed;
2. find and access needed visuals effectively and efficiently;
3. interpret and analyze the meanings of visuals;
4. evaluate visuals and their sources;
5. use visuals effectively;
6. design and create meaningful visuals; and
7. understand many of the ethical, legal, social, and economic issues surrounding the creation and use of visuals, and access and use visuals ethically.

These standards suggest that visual literacy is the ability to both "read" and "write" visuals. Even though visual literacy is not explicitly listed in many guidelines for curriculum requirements in higher education, there is a growing demand for teaching *information literacy*. The AAC&U explicitly lists information literacy in its *Essential Learning Outcomes* for liberal education and provides tactical guidance to educators with its *Information Literacy VALUE Rubric*. In disciplines with heavy emphasis on visuals—and I will argue astronomy is one of these—information literacy requires visual literacy.

Astronomy and Visual Literacy.   Because astronomy is inherently a visual science, it is a fertile academic discipline for the teaching and learning of visual literacy. For centuries, astronomers had to rely solely on the light that reaches Earth from space to figure out what was happening out there. Even now, with robots landing on other planets and moons in our solar system, it is the images of those worlds that captivate the public. Astronomy instructors make heavy use of visuals in class, both to inspire students and to convey our current understanding of the universe with visual metaphors and models.

A set of goals for introductory astronomy courses, established in 2003 by members of the American Astronomical Society (AAS), includes items related to content, skills, values, and attitude. Only a few of these directly ("how to make and use spatial/geometrical models") or indirectly ("critical thinking, including appropriate skepticism") relate to visual literacy. However, in their summary of the goals, Partridge and Greenstein (2003) noted that "[astronomy instructors] are lucky, when trying to reach non-science students, that astronomy has such a strong visual component. Students who find mathematics intimidating can enjoy the challenge of analyzing spatial-geometrical models" (51). They also offer the following advice:

> Teach from visual images. Astronomy is richly provided with compelling images. These have immediate appeal. More importantly, if we use them effectively, we can get students actively involved in forming scientific judgments on the bases of their own observations and thus improve their deductive skills. Having students look carefully at detailed images of the Martian surface, for instance, can help them frame arguments for the existence of a Martian atmosphere (airborne dust, sand dunes, and so on). (np)

While the ACRL visual literacy goals are different from the AAS goals, the examples I list in the rest of this chapter show how the two sets can complement each other. The quantity and diversity of visuals in astronomy can serve as useful examples for learning visual literacy.

Types of Visuals in Astronomy. Astronomers, like many scientists, rely on three basic types of visuals to convey information. Given the ubiquity of these and the tendency of scientists to classify nearly everything, it is surprising to me that my colleagues rarely discuss these three categories:

- *Images.* These are often photographs of an object, which may have been captured with a telescope or microscope. These may even be made using light that isn't visible to the human eye, including infrared light, ultraviolet light, and X-rays. Each pixel of an image represents a piece of data.
- *Diagrams.* These are simple or complex illustrations that *qualitatively* depict some process or system. These might include one or more images combined with graphics to convey some meaning.
- *Plots.* These are a form of diagram designed to convey *quantitative* information. Frequently, these are x–y plots showing how one variable changes with respect to another. Science professors often approach plots very differently from other diagrams since the former are used to communicate data. Thus, for this chapter I distinguish them as a separate category.

Figure 1.1. An Image, a Diagram, and a Plot from the Curiosity Rover on Mars

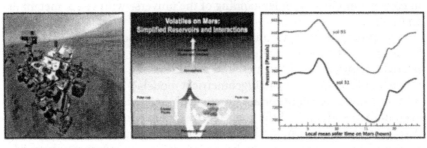

Source: NASA.

Any of these might be static, animated, or interactive. However, nearly all visuals in astronomy fall into one of these categories. Figure 1.1 shows three visuals from NASA press releases related to the Curiosity rover on Mars, with one image, one diagram, and one plot. In the subsequent sections, I will discuss examples of teaching students both to read and to write these three types of visuals.

Reading Visuals in Astronomy

Given that the majority of astronomy students learn in a lecture hall, it is common that students be required to interpret and analyze the meanings of visuals on slides, even if they are given no explicit instruction on how to do this. The authors of *Developing Visual Literacy in Science, K–8* (Vasquez, Comer, and Troutman 2010) acknowledge this and suggest that the "see-scan-analyze" thinking process is automatic, especially with photographic images. They propose that this process occurs "quickly and without cognitive effort" except for in young children and suggest that "[t]eachers must help [young children] develop the ability to reflect metacognitively (that is, think about what they are viewing and have a mental discourse about its relevance) so they can become visually literate" (5). Specifically, they recommend asking students follow-up questions after viewing a photograph, such as "What do you actually see in the photograph? What assumptions can you make or conclusions can you draw based on your observations? What feelings does the picture evoke for you?" (17).

Unfortunately, for many adult students, the process is *too* quick and has too little cognitive effort. In my own classes, I begin with standard techniques for teaching the reading of visuals (see Palmer, Chapter 2 of this volume). After showing students an astronomical image, without text or scale, I ask "What do you see with your eyes?" While they want to answer quickly ("Orion!" or "Jupiter!"), I have them list their most basic observations ("There are points of light." or "Some are red and a few are blue.")

before I let them start to draw inferences ("These are stars." or "The red ones are cooler.").

Learning to Read Images.   During the first week of class, students look at images of our planet, our Sun, our solar system, and then an image of a galaxy. Asking them what galaxy they see, a few quickly respond "The Milky Way" while a few others say "Andromeda." When I follow up with, "How can we take a picture of our own galaxy?" the students decide that it must be a picture of Andromeda, a nearby galaxy, since we can't see our own Milky Way Galaxy from the outside. I then ask them to sketch what the Andromeda Galaxy would look like from the inside and then compare this with images of the Milky Way as seen from Earth, and an artist's rendition of the Milky Way, based on astronomical data, created by Robert Hurt at Caltech. This image serves as a touchstone for the rest of the semester as we continually ask, "Who took the picture?" and "Is it a 'real' image or an illustration?"

Another example of students questioning image sources is the famous Hubble Space Telescope image of the Eagle Nebula. With its earthy color palette and organic shapes, it quickly became a public favorite. While the shapes are real, the colors in the photograph are not. The image uses artificial colors to emphasize details in the image and does not resemble what a human eye would actually see. True color photographs of the Eagle Nebula reveal that it is almost entirely pink, the color of hot hydrogen gas. While the astronomers describe the false color palette in their research paper, this caption is, for obvious reasons, never included on the T-shirts, coffee mugs, *Star Trek* episodes, or *USA Today* cover stories featuring the image. This serves as an example for students of how even a "real" image can mislead the reader when removed from the primary source.

Learning to Read Diagrams.   Astronomy textbooks are filled with colorful diagrams used to portray objects that are sometimes very big, very small, or just plain invisible. These diagrams become mental surrogates for a structure or system that humans cannot see. Unfortunately, the physical limitations of the printing process (or mistakes by the graphic artist) often lead to diagrams that are misleading.

For example, a very common misconception students have is that the phases of the Moon are caused by the shadow of the Earth. This likely occurs since students don't realize how infrequent such an alignment might be due to the sizes and distances involved. In reality, the distance to the Moon is thirty times the size of the Earth (or 3,000 percent) (see Figure 1.2). Taylor and Grundstrom (2011) found that in thirty middle school science textbooks, the distance from the Earth to the Moon was portrayed as only slightly larger than the size of the Earth (133 percent). Student estimates

Figure 1.2. The Earth–Moon System Represented to Scale

of this size were just a bit larger, matching the average seen in many online images describing the Earth–Moon system (200 percent). It seems probable that students' incorrect perceptions of this distance (and their subsequent impossible explanations for the phases of the Moon) are formed primarily from the bad textbook visuals.

Many students also have trouble understanding the cause of the seasons. This was highlighted in Schneps and Sadler's (1989) famous video on the topic, *A Private Universe*, in which they interviewed recent Harvard graduates. The film reveals a common misconception; many people know that the Earth is in an elliptical, not a circular, orbit and they use this fact to rationalize that summer must occur when the Earth is closer to the Sun. They do not realize that the Earth's orbit is *very* close to being circular; its actual distance from the Sun is at most 1.7 percent different from a perfect circular orbit. Many K–16 science books reinforce the incorrect beliefs by using diagrams with exaggerated elliptical orbits.

In both my astronomy classes for physics majors and nonmajors, students confirm that they believe the exaggerated elliptical orbits depicted in textbooks are real. When presented with various ellipses, they overwhelmingly pick highly eccentric options as closest to reality. When confronted with their own misconceptions during class, they eventually can answer this question correctly. In addition to teaching students the correct shape of Earth's orbit, this exercise also leads to discussion on perspective in images. Many chapter topics in astronomy textbooks (for example, the phases of the Moon, the cause of the seasons) involve diagrams shown from an oblique perspective, just slightly above the plane of the orbit. This makes even a true circle appear to be an oval.

Timothy Slater (2010), a prolific astronomy education researcher, developed "Metacognitive Visual Literacy Tasks" to scaffold the visual literacy in his own college astronomy classes. In each task, students are presented with a static visual, an open-ended question prompt, and three to six multiple-choice questions designed to guide them in understanding and using the visual. While my own class activities focus on small group discussions (up to thirty students), Slater's approach can be used with very large groups or with distance-learning students.

Learning to Read Plots.   Not all choices to use visuals by science professors are terribly sophisticated. All too often, novice instructors use visuals to "spice things up" in an otherwise dull lecture. One seasoned professor visiting my campus suggested adding random zombies to slides: "It will wake them up!" While there is little research on the impact zombie images have on student learning, I work under the supposition that they do not enhance the effectiveness of the underlying image.

An increasingly popular and effective approach among physics and astronomy educators is using interactive plots and diagrams to help students "experiment" with equations and concepts. Examples include the PhET simulations created by Nobel prizewinner Carl Wieman (Perkins et al.

2006), the Nebraska Astronomy Applet Project (Vogt, Cook, and Muise 2013), and Physlets (Christian and Belloni 2000). Class exercises using interactive PhET simulations have been shown to be more effective at helping students learn physics (electronic circuits, for example) than similar exercises using real lab equipment (Finkelstein et al. 2005).

In my own modern astrophysics course, we use Sloan Digital Sky Survey (SDSS) data throughout the semester. Tutorials for using these data are available through the SDSS Skyserver (Szalay et al. 2002). My exams are typically composed of just a few very basic questions that require students to interpret and analyze plots of real SDSS data. I have found that students are relatively comfortable inserting numbers into equations, but are less adept at gleaning those same numbers from plots. For example, the question "How hot is this star?" is quite easy for them to calculate if they are given the wavelength where the star is the brightest. However, when asked the same question and given a plot, they have difficulty extracting the peak wavelength from it. Teaching students to analyze real spectral data plots of stars (with noise, biases, and so on) rather than simplified illustrations of spectra has become a deliberate activity in my classes after having had students fail at these tasks on exams.

Writing Visuals in Astronomy

An increasing number of college instructors assign writing-to-learn assignments rather than traditional essays (Newell 2008). This same approach can be applied in astronomy classes by having students "write" images, diagrams, and plots to learn science concepts.

Learning to Write Images.   To many people, "writing" images is photography. The exponential rise in popularity of mobile devices over the past decade has led to an increase in the percentage of college students with cameras on their person at all times. In 2013, the Pew Research Center reported that 56 percent of American adults owned a smartphone, up from 35 percent in 2011. For college-aged students (18–24), 79 percent had a smartphone with a camera (Smith 2013).

Capturing photographs of celestial objects provides several interesting challenges that standard smartphone photography does not. Celestial targets are often too small or too faint to be photographed without special apps to approximate longer exposures (for example, the *Night Modes* app for the iPhone). The sky also moves slowly (360° every 24 hours) such that deep exposures require the camera to be on a mount that can track the sky. Attempting to have students in Astronomy 101 use their own cameras teaches them the limitations of these devices.

In Elon's 200-level astronomy class, students begin using special black-and-white cameras specifically designed for astrophotography. To create color images, they must combine images taken through three filters (red, green, and blue) using simple image processing software such as SalsaJ

(Faye and Faye 2009). This teaches them the techniques professional astronomers use when creating color images with the Hubble Space Telescope and other facilities. It also reinforces the ability to expertly read astronomical images (for example, the false-color Eagle nebula) since they know how the proverbial sausage is made.

Learning to Write Diagrams.   In physics classes with emphasis on peer instruction, it is increasingly common for students to work problems in groups of three using small whiteboards (Beichner and Saul 2003), cut from cheap "shower board" available at most big box hardware stores. When my colleague, Claudine Moreau, brought whiteboards to her *Introduction to Astronomy* survey class, she had the students use them in a different way. While physics students tend to use the boards to work through mathematical problems, her astronomy classes more frequently used the boards to sketch out astronomy visuals (see Figure 1.3).

Moreau originally intended for the whiteboards to be used to stimulate discussions of the assigned reading. At first, student groups did not take "drawing" seriously, spending more time embellishing their responses with cartoons than answering the question. However, as the semester progressed, they treated it like a regular part of the class. Student sketches would be displayed at the front of the room and critiqued by the class. Over time, this process improved their design of visuals. This approach also allowed Moreau to quickly assess at a glance the progress of each student group as they worked on their responses.

Figure 1.3. Student Whiteboard Sketches of Eclipses

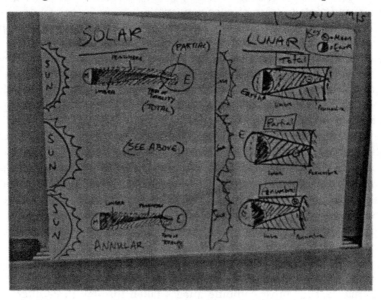

Source: Claudine Moreau, *Introduction to Astronomy* class at Elon University.

NEW DIRECTIONS FOR TEACHING AND LEARNING • DOI: 10.1002/tl

Learning to Write Plots.   Whereas creating scientific images and diagrams requires an understanding of the science, creating scientific plots involves an understanding of both the science and essential math skills. Students often have difficulties understanding basic x–y scatter plots of data. This is especially problematic if one or both of the scales are logarithmic (1, 10, 100, 1,000, and so on) rather than linear (1, 2, 3, 4, and so on). To improve their ability to both read and write such plots, I have them begin with Google Motion Charts preloaded with astronomical data. For example, students studying the debate over the definition of a planet use a chart with data for Pluto, the planets, and several smaller objects orbiting the Sun (Crider 2011). They can easily switch back and forth between linear and log scales to see why the latter might be necessary when plotting data that span a large range.

Students in my 300-level astronomy class go a step further and make plots using Microsoft Excel or the programming language Python (with the *matplotlib* plotting package). Since the default settings in Microsoft Excel are not conducive to making clear, scientific plots, I typically have several "studio" days where students create and revise a plot until it meets the publication standards of astronomy research journals. Beginner-level exercises involve finding and correcting five errors inserted into a spreadsheet (or the plotting code) until they reproduce a plot projected at the front of the room. Intermediate-level exercises require students to create a plot from scratch, given a common data set. For a final exam, students must collect their own data, create their own meaningful plots, and describe their results in a short paper. To teach students the basic principles used for visualizing quantitative data, I recommend books by Stephen Few (2009; with Excel examples) and Nathan Yau (2011; with R examples), as well as classics by Edward Tufte (2003).

Synthesizing Visuals into Presentations

The ability to read and write images, diagrams, and plots is clearly a critical skill for astronomers and a valuable one for students. The examples above show how I have attempted to foster visual literacy in my own classes. However, using these skills in combination has produced the most growth in my students. In nearly every course I teach, students are required to work with me in creating their own ten-to-fifteen-minute slide presentations for the class. This starts with a ten-element rubric to guide crafting of both their oral and visual stories. One item on this rubric grades the graphic design itself.

1 point: the slides caused physical discomfort to the audience.
2 points: the slides had excessive text, mismatched bullet points, or low-resolution images.
3 points: the slides obviously used a built-in template.

**Figure 1.4. Student Slides before (Left) and after (Right)
Instructor Meetings**

Sources: NASA, Slides produced by students.

4 points: visuals were all high resolution with little text. Text-only slides
were easy to read. Appropriate color palettes were used.
5 points: the graphic design of the slides was "prize worthy."

It also includes one or more mandatory rehearsals during my office
hours. These conversations naturally involve discussion of the content itself and improvements they can make to the story arc of their talk. I also
regularly coach students on "slidecraft" and the appropriate use of visuals.
The example in Figure 1.4 shows how one particular student group used
a template-based slide to describe the methane lakes on Saturn's moon, Titan, before such a conversation. After our meeting, the group used just two
images: one of Titan and one of the lakes.

Much of my own advice stems from the writings of Edward Tufte, who
argues that the templates within PowerPoint™ encourage speakers to write
with "bullets" instead of complete sentences and to show low-resolution images (or worse yet, clip-art) alongside them rather than high-resolution data
(Tufte 2003). A contrasting but effective alternative is the "Lessig Method"
of presentation used by Stanford Law Professor, Larry Lessig, which uses
slides with minimal content that change rapidly to keep pace with the verbal content. More recently, Pecha Kucha (twenty minutes, slides change every twenty seconds) and the Ignite slideshow formula (five minutes, slides
change automatically every fifteen seconds) have become popular formats
to guide students (and professors) in structuring talks to match the impact
of the Lessig Method.

Conclusion: Visual Literacy as a Component of
Information Literacy

Student responses to the FOX "Conspiracy Theory" video prompted me
to seriously reconsider the goals for my astronomy classes. Ultimately, I decided to emphasize visual and information literacy skills over content deliv-
ery. In addition to the activities already described, I assigned some projects
to explicitly address the arguments made by the Moon hoax believers.

Often this meant evaluating visuals and their sources. For example, the FOX video argued that the Moon landing photos released by NASA were "too good": every Apollo mission photo was perfectly framed, which is an impossible result if the cameras were chest-mounted on the astronauts. When my students sifted through the full archive of NASA images, they discovered thousands of images, but only a few of the best ones were selected for use by the press. The FOX video also used an edited video clip showing the American flag flapping, allegedly due to "wind," and claimed that this is evidence of a conspiracy because everyone knows that there is no "wind" on the Moon. Students watching the full video quickly found that the flag only moved when astronauts touched the pole it was mounted on.

In addition to leading them through a deeper "reading" of the FOX visuals, I had students "write" their own visuals to debunk the conspiracy theory. For example, the FOX video claimed that photos of the lunar lander should have stars in the background, that all of the shadows should be perpendicular since there was a single light source—the Sun—and that the video of the astronauts' lunar gait was identical to that of humans walking on Earth but played at half speed. With their own cameras, groups of students easily developed videos showing each claim to be completely incorrect.

Ultimately, this lengthy and engaged process convinced most, but not all, of my students that the documentary's claims were misleading. Even after the students presented the results of their experiments to each other, only 90 percent of them believed that humans landed on the Moon, which is exactly where I started! I could undo the damage from the video, but could not yet convince the original 10 percent that clung to the conspiracy. Eventually, two television shows with their own well-produced visuals, a National Geographic documentary and an episode of Penn and Teller's *Bullshit!*, finally convinced them all.

To counter the misleading visuals used in "edutainment" (and sometimes in education, as we've seen), students and teachers must find and create equally powerful visuals, including photos, diagrams, plots, presentations, and videos. With the exponentially growing amount of visual content that our students will face throughout their lives, teaching them to respond to it with visual and information literacy skills is a clear priority for liberal education.

References

Association of American Colleges and Universities (AAC&U). 2005. *Liberal Education Outcomes*. http://archive.aacu.org/leap/pdfs/LEAP_Report_FINAL.pdf.

Beichner, R. J., and J. M. Saul. 2003, July. "Introduction to the SCALE-UP (Student-Centered Activities for Large Enrollment Undergraduate Programs) Project." Paper presented at The International School of Physics "Enrico Fermi," Varenna, Italy.

Christian, W., and M. Belloni. 2000. *Physlets*. Upper Saddle River, NJ: Prentice Hall.

Crider, A. 2011. "Debating Pluto: Searching for the Classroom of the Future and Ending up in the Past." *Astronomy Beat* 74: 1–6.

Faye, S., and M. Faye. 2009. "Teaching Astronomy and Astrophysics with Hands-on-Universe and SalsaJ: Stars, Planets, Exoplanets and Dark Matter." *Proceedings of the International Astronomical Union* 5 (S260): 715–719.

Few, S. 2009. *Now You See It: Simple Visualization Techniques for Quantitative Analysis.* Burlingame, CA: Analytics Press.

Finkelstein, N. D., W. K. Adams, C. J. Keller, P. B. Kohl, K. K. Perkins, N. S. Podolefsky, S. Reid, and R. LeMaster. 2005. "When Learning about the Real World Is Better Done Virtually: A Study of Substituting Computer Simulations for Laboratory Equipment." *Physical Review Special Topics—Physics Education Research* 1 (1). doi:10.1103/PhysRevSTPER.1.010103.

Hattwig, D., J. Burgess, K. Bussert, and A. Medaille. 2011. *Visual Literacy Competency Standards for Higher Education.* Chicago, IL: Association of College & Research Libraries.

Kelsen, K. 2010. *Unleashing the Power of Digital Signage: Content Strategies for the 5th Screen.* Florence, KY: Taylor & Francis.

Little, D., P. Felten, and C. Berry. 2010. "Liberal Education in a Visual World." *Liberal Education* 96 (2): 44–49.

Newell, G. E. 2008. "Writing to Learn." In *Handbook of Writing Research*, edited by C. A. MacArthur, S. Graham, and J. Fitzgerald, 235–247. New York, NY: The Guilford Press.

Partridge, B., and G. Greenstein. 2003. "Goals for 'Astro 101': Report on Workshops for Department Leaders." *Astronomy Education Review* 2: 46–89.

Perkins, K., W. Adams, M. Dubson, N. Finkelstein, S. Reid, C. Wieman, and R. LeMaster. 2006. "PhET: Interactive Simulations for Teaching and Learning Physics." *The Physics Teacher* 44: 18–23.

Schneps, M., and P. Sadler. 1989. *A Private Universe* [Video]. Santa Monica, CA: Pyramid Film and Video.

Slater, T. F. 2010. "Engaging Student's Astronomical Thinking with Metacognitive Literacy Tasks." *The Physics Teacher* 48 (9): 618–619.

Smith, A. 2013. *Smartphone Ownership—2013 Update.* Washington, DC: Pew Research Center.

Szalay, A. S., J. Gray, A. R. Thakar, P. Z. Kunszt, T. Malik, J. Raddick, C. Stoughton, and J. vandenBerg. 2002. "The SDSS Skyserver: Public Access to the Sloan Digital Sky Server Data." In *Proceedings of the 2002 ACM SIGMOD International Conference on Management of Data*, edited by D. DeWitt, 570–581. New York, NY: ACM.

Taylor, R. S., and E. D. Grundstrom. 2011. "Diagrammatic Representational Constraints of Spatial Scale in Earth–Moon System Astronomy Instruction." *Astronomy Education Review* 10. doi:10.3847/AER2009075.

Tufte, E. R. 2003. *The Cognitive Style of PowerPoint*, Vol. 2006. Cheshire, CT: Graphics Press.

Vasquez, J. A., M. W. Comer, and F. H. Troutman. 2010. *Developing Visual Literacy in Science, K–8.* Arlington, VA: NSTA Press.

Vogt, N. P., S. P. Cook, and A. S. Muise. 2013. "A New Resource for College Distance Education Astronomy Laboratory Exercises." *American Journal of Distance Education* 27 (3): 189–200.

Yau, N. 2011. *Visualize This: The FlowingData Guide to Design, Visualization, and Statistics.* Indianapolis, IN: Wiley.

ANTHONY CRIDER *is a professor of astronomy in the Department of Physics at Elon University.*

This chapter describes a first-year seminar course designed to develop students' visual literacy skills. After a brief overview of the course and a discussion of the evidence supporting the efficacy of the instructional interventions, a timeline and description of the specific learning activities are presented.

Learning to See the Infinite: Teaching Visual Literacy in a First-Year Seminar Course

Michael S. Palmer

Little, Felten, and Barry (2010) have argued that "visual literacy... is a critical skill for twenty-first-century students and ought to be a central component of liberal education" (46). They go on to suggest that instructors teaching courses in academic disciplines outside those commonly affiliated with visual literacy (for example, art history and media studies) and those teaching first-year general education through capstone courses should explicitly help students develop the ability to interpret, negotiate, and make meaning from information presented in an image. This is not only because images saturate our daily lives but also because many fields, including those in the arts, sciences, social sciences, and health sciences, rely heavily on images as data sources and require a heightened level of visual literacy to understand and interpret the world.

First-year seminar courses are ideal places within curricula to embed this essential skill (Barefoot 1992). The content of such courses, though important, often only serves as a backdrop. It is the hook, the thing that "tricks" students into thinking that they are learning about the origins of the universe or the Wild West when in fact they are developing lifelong skills such as critical thinking, creative thinking, close reading, and visual literacy.

In 2009, I developed and taught a first-year seminar course, and its hook was infinity. This highly interdisciplinary, discussion-based course,

---

I kindly acknowledge Tatiana Matthews for help with the analysis of the pre-/postassessment data. I am forever grateful to Deandra Little for introducing me to the world of visual literacy, for mentoring me throughout the project, and for her uncommon collegiality.

NEW DIRECTIONS FOR TEACHING AND LEARNING, no. 141, Spring 2015 © 2015 Wiley Periodicals, Inc.
Published online in Wiley Online Library (wileyonlinelibrary.com) • DOI: 10.1002/tl.20119

called Falling from Infinity (FFI), drew on a diverse set of perspectives—literary, poetic, artistic, mathematical, scientific, religious, philosophical—and invited students to spend a semester grappling with uncountable numbers, immeasurable spaces, and unending times. Visual literacy skills were taught throughout the semester through formal instruction and a series of carefully designed learning activities. This chapter briefly describes the evolution of the course, highlights the qualitative and quantitative evidence demonstrating the development of students' visual literacy skills, and lays out the general sequence of the in- and out-of-class activities, all of which can be implemented in a variety of courses.

Overview

Throughout the semester, I encourage students in FFI to think critically about how people in different disciplines imagine infinity and to begin to shape and creatively express their own views of the concept. The first time I taught the course (spring 2009), we began early in the semester exploring works of art with the following question in mind: "Do these works have anything to do with the infinite?" This question implicitly asks students to make meaningful observations and then use their observations to make a claim. The first works we discussed were relatively straightforward lithographs of M. C. Escher. When I asked students to discuss the connections between these works and the infinite, I naively expected them to respond in one of two ways: "Yes, the piece explores aspects of the infinite because . . . " or "No, it has nothing to do with infinity because . . . " Instead, students responded subjectively with comments such as, "I think the painting is about . . . " or "I believe the artist was trying to say"; the phrases filling in the blanks were—at best—only tangentially related to the artwork we were discussing. Students simply were not prepared to discuss art or images in ways they might a text, that is, critically. In an ad hoc fashion, I adjusted the course to include several exercises to help students *see* the works of art we were encountering. For instance, I began by displaying an image not associated with infinity and asked students to go through the following steps in answer to the question, "What do you see in this image?":

- First, spend two minutes writing down all of your observations.
- Next, turn to your neighbor, compare observations, and add any observations you may have missed.
- Then, based on your observations, make a claim to answer the question. Your claim should take the form, "I infer ____ because of [observation(s) ____]."

With a variety of learning activities, we proceeded in a similar fashion throughout the semester, always focusing first on their observations before making claims supported by the observations.

NEW DIRECTIONS FOR TEACHING AND LEARNING • DOI: 10.1002/tl

Curious as to the effect of these interventions on my students' ability to make meaning of images, I collected some preliminary data in the form of end-of-course evaluations. To the statement, "Because of this course, I am better able to critically analyze visual images," students respond on average 4.40 out of 5.00 (5 = strongly agree). Select qualitative comments included:

> The most important skill I learned [in this course] was analyzing works of art (painting/photography). (FFI student, spring 2009)

> ...every time I look at a painting now, I'll think: (1) Observation! (2) Inference. (FFI student, spring 2009)

With this information in hand, I systematically modified FFI, making visual literacy another explicit objective of the course and systematically incorporating a series of learning activities designed to foster this cognitive skill. I taught the revised course during the fall of 2009. In addition to collecting end-of-course evaluation data similar to that gathered during the first iteration of the course, I measured the effects of these interventions using a pre-/postsemester methodology where my students ($n = 16$) were asked to look at two different, but stylistically similar, paintings and write a response to the following two questions: What do you see? And, what do you think it means? The paintings were Salvador Dali's *The Persistence of Memory* and *The Disintegration of the Persistence of Memory*.

Students' responses were analyzed using Toulmin's argument model (Toulmin 1969), with particular focus on claim, supporting evidence, and warrant (that is, the inferences or assumptions taken for granted by the writer that connect the claim and the supporting evidence). Supporting evidence was defined as the observations—basic and advanced—that students made. A basic observation described an object or feature of the painting without significant qualifiers. An advanced observation described an object or feature of the painting beyond merely identifying it, such as the position of the object/feature relative to others or its location relative to the painting (for example, foreground/background); the texture of objects or the texture of the painting itself; the contrast or juxtaposition of objects or features; the source and/or direction of light; a minute, easily overlooked detail of the piece; or an observation the viewer made about her own experience viewing the painting (for example, "I looked at the objects in the painting in a counterclockwise manner."). The number and quality of observations, the number and strength of claims, and strengths of the warrants were analyzed.

Although a thorough discussion of the results of this study is beyond the scope of this chapter, the data suggest that the classroom interventions significantly improved my students' ability to make detailed and nuanced observations in the images we explored and to develop stronger claims supported by their observations. For example, at the start of the semester, before any instructional interventions, the median values for the number of basic observations and advanced observations made were 13.0 (range = 0–33) and 2.0 (range = 0–7), respectively, and students provided 2.5 pieces of evidence for their best-supported claim (range = 0–6). The strength of their warrant was generally weak to moderate. Near the end of the semester, following most instructional interventions, the median values for the number of basic observations and advanced observations made were 26.0 (range = 13–68) and 3.0 (range = 2–14), respectively, and students provided 8.0 pieces of visual evidence for their best-supported claim (range = 3–40). The strength of their warrant was generally moderate to strong (Palmer 2012).

Because I embedded numerous learning activities focused on improving visual literacy skills throughout the course, it is difficult to pinpoint which activities had the greatest impact on my students' learning. A portion of every class period, whether explicitly or implicitly, was devoted to some aspect of visual literacy. Most likely, it was the sum of activities that led to the positive gains rather than any one particular intervention. To give a sense of these activities, in terms of timing and complexity, I provide next a timeline of the course that highlights the basic pedagogical interventions and expounds on a few of the activities that challenged students to think about images in new or nuanced ways. The sequence of these activities could easily be adapted to other first-year seminar courses, and parts of the sequence would be appropriate for more advanced, discipline-based courses.

Timeline of Visual Literacy Activities

The visual literacy activities described next are presented in chronological order so as to make the scaffolding apparent. I planned them to help students develop foundational visual literacy skills early in the semester to support more complex ones later on. To help clarify the order, I've denoted the weeks of the semester using an A–Z labeling scheme.

Many of the visual literacy learning activities were developed in class through small-group, collaborative exercises or large-group discussions. Others were assigned as part of reflective journal assignments. For the latter, students completed a short task related to course content outside of class and then wrote a 1- to 2-page reflection on the experience. For example, students were asked to look at images outside of class and briefly reflect on how this new information complicated their understanding of the infinite. Other activities supported more complex assignments, such as creating a photo essay and writing a 3- to 4-page reflection evaluating the ways the photo was effective in representing the infinite and in what ways it fell short.

NEW DIRECTIONS FOR TEACHING AND LEARNING • DOI: 10.1002/tl

Week A.   During class, I showed my students Ed Miracle's painting *Beyond Forever* and asked them to discuss the following questions in small groups:

- What is your initial reaction to this work of art?
- What aspect(s) of the infinite is the artist trying to convey? In what ways is he successful? In what ways is he not?
- In your opinion, what are the limitations of representing infinity in such a way?

The follow-up, large-group discussion was entirely student-led. I offered very little commentary, hoping that students would begin to feel comfortable talking about art/images without fear of judgment from an authority figure.

After the first class meeting, I invited all the students to meet with me in small groups outside of class. During those meetings, I asked students to email me their responses to the following prompt before the next class period: Look at Salvador Dali's painting *The Persistence of Memory* and answer the following two questions:

1. What do you see in the painting?
2. What do you think the painting means?

Since this was to serve as a preassessment of my students' ability to make observations and support a claim, there was no follow-up to this exercise.

Week B.   I asked students to look at several M. C. Escher pieces (*Regular Division of the Plane #70*; *Smaller and Smaller*; *Circle Limit I*; *Circle Limit III*; *Circle Limit IV*) before class. During the in-class, large-group discussion, I implicitly introduced the ideas of observation, analysis, and reaction. Questions asked during the discussion included:

- What are your initial reactions?
- Does the piece evoke any emotion?
- Where is your eye initially drawn? Now, what do you see?
- What might you infer from these observations?
- If this were your first encounter with "infinity," what would you have learned?

Again, I offered very little commentary. I simply wanted to get students to realize that there are multiple ways to look at an image, some more strongly grounded in the visual evidence than others.

Week C.   I asked my students to look at several other M. C. Escher pieces (*Snakes*; *Path of Life II*; *Whirlpools*) before class. I began our in-class, large-group discussion by reviewing the Escher works we discussed during our previous meeting. I then demonstrated, using a think-aloud approach,

NEW DIRECTIONS FOR TEACHING AND LEARNING • DOI: 10.1002/tl

the process of observation and analysis (without defining either the terms or the process skills of observation and analysis) for the lithograph *Whirlpools*. After making a claim and supporting it with my observations, I asked students "Do you have an alternate analysis of this work of art?" and made them provide evidence to support their analysis.

Next, I asked students to make observations of *Path of Life II*, individually writing their observations down first and then sharing these with a classmate to see if they missed anything. Then I asked the following questions as part of a large-group discussion:

- Keeping my example analysis of *Whirlpools* in mind—an analysis that may be completely wrong—comment on *Path of Life II*. How does this particular work change/improve upon/detract from Escher's depiction of limits?
- Based on what you got out of today's preclass reading, what kind of infinity is Escher depicting?
- Do these works tell us anything about infinity?

For each of these questions, I prompted students to support their arguments with the concrete observations they made earlier.

Week D.   At this point in the semester, students were beginning to learn the importance of observations and how these strengthen a claim. What they had not yet realized though was how observations can be clouded by personal prejudices and biases. To help them recognize this, I engaged them in the following in-class exercise: First, I gave each student a blank piece of white copy paper and an eraserless lead pencil and asked them to "draw your yesterday," to capture what their day looked like visually. On the back of the paper, I instructed them to write up to five adjectives that described their day. Then, one by one a handful of volunteers displayed their drawings, while the other students tried to guess what the artist's day was like; that is, what adjectives they wrote on the back of their drawing. The class supported their claims about each artist's day with observations from the drawing. What students quickly realized was that the common, everyday symbols each person used to draw their day (for example, computers, books, and smiley faces) meant different things to different people. The symbols were shaping their "observations." In the end, students were generally unsuccessful at guessing the adjectives that described each artist's day. Next, I gave the students another blank piece of paper, but this time instructed them to draw their yesterday without using any readily recognizable symbols. I again asked them to list up to five adjectives on the back of the paper that described their day. The session of "guess what the student's day was like" that followed was dramatically different from the first. Using only observations of line shape and stroke, lead density, and placement of these elements on the paper, students were able to quite accurately describe each artist's day. Simply put, students were better able to make objective observations when they were dealing with unrecognizable symbols.

During this week, students also completed a photo essay assignment. I asked them to take at least one digital picture that captured—in their mind's eye—some element of the infinite. They had complete freedom to choose which aspect of the infinite to explore as well as the subject of their photos. For example, they could explore numbers, time, or space, and produce a photograph of a nature scene or a still life. Along with their photo(s), they submitted a 3- to 4-page reflective essay describing what they were attempting to capture on film, in what ways the photo was effective in representing the infinite, and in what ways it fell short. Here, in this assignment, the students' claim was defined; their photo(s) captured some aspect of the infinite. Their reflection, therefore, asked them to support this claim using observations from their photo(s).

Week E.   As part of a preclass reflection journal assignment, I asked students to look at two of their classmates' photos (see photo essay assignment, Week D) and suggested they respond to the following questions: What are your initial reactions to your classmate's photo? Do you see infinity in it? How does it uniquely capture the infinite? What are the limitations? During the next class period, students met in small groups and shared their feedback with each other.

Week F.   Building on the drawing exercise described above (see Week D), students looked at Caspar David Friedrich's painting *Monk by the Sea* before class. In class, I asked them to respond to the question, "What do you see?" I then asked them to individually write down three to five adjectives that described their *emotional* response to the painting. Afterward, they shared these in the large group as I wrote and categorized their adjectives on the board. This particular painting is unique in that it typically evokes polar opposite responses: some viewers feel it evokes "awe" and a feeling of "tranquility," while others feel it evokes "dread" and "hopelessness." During the conversation, I asked the students, "What in the painting leads you to feel...?" After all responses were collected and reported out on the board, we discussed the question, "Which set of responses is correct?" What my students discovered through this activity is that some claims, when based solely on the observational data alone, are more easily supported than others.

As part of their reflection journal assignment, students compared Friedrich's *Monk by the Sea* and Vincent van Gogh's *Starry Night* and responded to the questions: What are the similarities and differences in what you see? What are the similarities and differences in your emotional responses to the paintings? I suggested they use a double-column entry to help with the comparison.

Week G.   With much of the visual literacy foundation laid, I began this week to formally define certain terms, like observation (a neutral, nonjudgmental, and verifiable statement) and inference (a meaning, an interpretation, or an assumption based on observation), and to systematically engage my students in critical analysis of the images we were encountering. I began our in-class discussion by displaying only a portion of Joel Sternfeld's photograph *Warren Avenue at 23rd Street, Detroit, Michigan*. I choose this particular photo, one that has nothing to do with infinity, to avoid having students overlay their prejudices and biases about infinity. They were first prompted to make as many observations about the visible part of the photograph as possible, preceding each observation with the statement "I see..." Next, I revealed another portion of the photograph and asked them to add to their list of observations. I continued to reveal the photograph slowly, piece by piece, until the image was complete. Once the students were satisfied that they made all relevant observations, they were then prompted to make inferences, beginning each with "I infer...because..." In follow-up questions, I prompted them to consider the strength of their inferences, asking "How well supported is your inference based on the observations we just made?"

After this exercise, students returned to van Gogh's *Starry Night*, and again individually wrote down all their observations, compared notes with their neighbor, created a combined class list, and then made the best-supported inferences possible.

Week H.   As a more in-depth assignment, students wrote a creative short story no longer than ten pages centered around one of the following two paintings: Van Gogh's *At Eternity's Gate* or Ed Miracle's *Emma*. I encouraged students to begin their story with the scene depicted in the painting, end it with the scene, or let the story encompass the scene. The assessment rubric highlighted critical analysis of the painting: Integration of the "story" of the painting—inferred from accurate and thorough observation—within the short story is seamless, appropriate, and compelling.

In a two-stage, in-class activity building on the drawing exercise described in Week D, students used fingerpaints to depict abstract words to help them better understand how an image creator can influence a viewer by the choices she makes. Guidelines included:

1. Choose one of the following words to draw: everything, nothing, eternity, oblivion. Write your name and word on the back of the canvas.
2. Paint your word without using recognizable symbols. Fill the canvas. Use at least three colors. You only have twenty minutes; don't think too much.
3. Take your painting home and see if you can get a few friends who are not in the class to guess your word. Have them explain what in the painting makes them think of a particular word. Using their feedback, repaint your word—using the same basic motif—but try to improve upon it.

The second stage of this activity was completed in Week I (see next).

Lastly, for their reflection journal, students completed the postassessment activity: "In lieu of a journal entry this week, use your developing visual analysis skills to look closely at *The Disintegration of the Persistence of Time* and answer the following two questions:

1. What do you see in the painting?
2. What do you think the painting means?"

Week I.   At the start of the class period, we completed the fingerpainting exercise (Week H) framed as follows: "As an artist, once you make your work public, it's no longer what you think that matters, it's what the viewer thinks. But, a viewer can't interpret it any way she wishes; her analysis must be grounded in her observations. Thus, you have some control in directing the viewer to see what you see. Let's see what viewers of your art see." The exercise unfolded as such:

1. Students chose their "best" painting from their two attempts.
2. Students split into three groups and gave each group another's paintings. The groups were tasked with grouping the paintings by word (that is, everything, nothing, eternity, immortality), without looking at the titles on the back. Using sticky notes, students labeled each grouping and listed out the qualities each painting in the group had in common. In other words, "What do you see that makes you think of...?" I suggested to students that they may need to regroup paintings after their initial categorizations.
3. Then, as a large group, we looked at all the like-grouped paintings (for example, all the eternity paintings) and discussed whether each painting belonged. As the conversation progressed, the students chose to move a few paintings between groups according to class consensus.
4. Finally, each artist revealed the word he or she had painted.

Remarkably, students were able to accurately label fifteen of the sixteen paintings! The one painting they missed elicited the most discussion, with some arguing that the painting depicted eternity, while others argued immortality. Later the student artist revealed she was struggling with how to paint eternity and felt it looked more like immortality. Clearly, my students were able to utilize their burgeoning visual literacy skills to analyze a set of abstract paintings with a high degree of precision and accuracy.

We then turned our attention to some of the more nuanced observations one can make about an image. I guided students in comparing Dali's *The Persistence of Memory* and *The Disintegration of the Persistence of Memory,* focusing their attention on elements such as line, shape, color, space, texture, size, time of day, sense of distance, and viewer's eye movement.

NEW DIRECTIONS FOR TEACHING AND LEARNING • DOI: 10.1002/tl

Week J.   During this last week, students looked at Vincent van Gogh's *At Eternity's Gate* before class. In class, I showed students an earlier drawing of the painting and asked them, "What is the expectation of eternity in these two pieces? How are they the same? How are they different? Why?" Now, with a number of visual literacy skills at their disposal, I pushed students to make more detailed and nuanced observations and better supported claims.

Summary

Because the course provided a variety of creative learning activities devoted to visual literacy, students were able to move beyond merely glancing at an image and having a subjective reaction to it to carefully seeing an image and responding critically to it. The qualitative and quantitative course data described in the overview provide compelling evidence to that fact. In a number of ways, the learning environment I created not only kept my students engaged in the cognitively difficult task of visual analysis but also inspired them to continue to develop visual literacy skills. As one student wrote in his final learning portfolio,

> This class has taught me something that no class has before: how to analyze and infer paintings for myself... Before [this class], I just looked at art. If it didn't look "cool" or "interesting" to me, I would just continue on. I'm not going to lie, I went to the van Gogh museum in Amsterdam this [past] summer, and although I probably spent a good hour or so in there, the maximum amount of time I looked at any one painting was probably 30 seconds tops... I truly believe that without this class I would have continued to go on and just take Friedrich's "Monk by the Sea" for what it is, a monk by the sea. But now I see the dark sky and water, the white tips on the waves and the curved coast line... (FFI student, fall 2009).

Because there were very few content-focused learning objectives in my first-year seminar course, concentrating on an essential skill like visual literacy was relatively easy. And, because the content was centered around relevant, intriguing, or provocative questions, my students seemed willing to persist in developing the skill. Given the general approaches I adopted for teaching visual literacy, it is not unreasonable to think that instructors teaching similar first-year seminars or even other disciplinary courses could adapt all or some of the activities to fit within the context of their courses. And, these instructors might reasonably see similar learning gains and positive student perceptions about the learning experience.

References

Barefoot, B. O. 1992. "Helping First-Year College Students Climb the Academic Ladder: Report of a National Survey of Freshman Seminar Programming in American Higher Education." PhD diss., College of William and Mary.

Little, D., P. Felten, and C. Berry. 2010. "Liberal Education in a Visual World." *Liberal Education* 96 (2): 44–49.

Palmer, M. S. 2012, February. "Learning to See the Infinite: Teaching and Measuring Visual Literacy." Paper presented at the Annual Conference on Higher Education Pedagogy, Blacksburg, VA.

Toulmin, S. E. 1969. *The Uses of Argument*. Cambridge, UK: Cambridge University Press.

MICHAEL S. PALMER is associate professor and associate director of the University of Virginia's Teaching Resource Center and lecturer in chemistry.

3

This chapter describes how photography can inspire and cultivate sociological mindfulness. One set of assignments uses self-portraiture to highlight the complexity of visual representations of social identity. Another uses photography to guide sociological inquiry. Both sets of assignments draw on the Literacy Through Photography methodology, using the interplay of image making and writing to foster creativity and insight and strengthen communication and observation skills.

Sociology through Photography

Katherine Hyde

Over four decades ago, the artist Wendy Ewald began a fascinating endeavor, teaching children around the world how to use the camera to express their own life stories. Ewald developed a methodology called Literacy Through Photography (LTP), which integrates photography and writing through assignments that explore such universal themes as self, family, community, and dreams (Ewald and Lightfoot 2001). LTP assignments focus on the elements of timing, framing, point of view, and the use of symbol and details, which are essential to both photography and writing. Students learn to translate their abstract visions, interests, and feelings into visual form (Hyde 2005). Likewise, children's pictures inspire their writing. The concrete details in photos provide an easy springboard for writing, and students' confidence in their writing is bolstered by their familiarity with, even expertise about, their subjects—whether their backyard, the graffiti on their street, a church service, a family meal, the posters on a bedroom wall, a grandmother's kitchen, the Honduran flag hanging on a doorstep, a younger sister's piano lesson, or a favorite skateboarding move.

Like many others, I am inspired by the insight and complexity of children's visual and written representations and intrigued by the implications of centering overlooked voices/visions—whether in the classroom, the art world, or in the fields of documentary and ethnography. Working locally and internationally with teachers and students on LTP projects for the past ten years has also convinced me to place photography at the heart of my undergraduate teaching—to teach sociology *through* photography. My students learn how the everyday pictures they see and post on Facebook and Instagram contain rich information about the social world; they learn how

NEW DIRECTIONS FOR TEACHING AND LEARNING, no. 141, Spring 2015 © 2015 Wiley Periodicals, Inc.
Published online in Wiley Online Library (wileyonlinelibrary.com) • DOI: 10.1002/tl.20120

31

to ask sociological questions when looking at photographs, how to make pictures with a sociological eye, and how to communicate abstract and theoretical concepts visually.

Overview

In this chapter, I describe two ways I utilize photography in undergraduate education—as a tool for self-expression and reflection and as a tool to guide inquiry in sociology courses.

I first describe a self-portrait assignment that connects self-expression with an exploration of social identity and visual representation. The assignment serves the obvious purpose of introducing students of LTP to the methodology they will in turn teach in local classrooms. More broadly, it requires students to envision and create a self-portrait through a thoughtful, reflexive, multistage process—one that highlights the choices made in crafting representations of self and that considers how others read our constructions. Students likewise consider the relative power of various social groups to control their own image, counter misrepresentations, and contextualize their portrayal in popular media, historical accounts, and so forth. The exercises slow down the making, "publishing," and distributing of images—which is countercultural, but worthwhile in an era of ever-popular "selfies," the presentation anxieties of maintaining an online avatar (Turkle 2011), and the sweeping implications of new technologies such as Google Glass. Students' portraits are invitations to deep thinking and powerful written pieces. More than learning to write, students are writing to learn—about themselves, their classmates, self–society connections, and the slippery truth of representations.

In the second section, the assignments I describe use photography as a tool to guide sociological inquiry. Students learn to think of photographs as data—whether looking at treasured family pictures or ordinary shots documenting people, places, and objects. They learn to pay attention to the complex and nuanced implications of the familiar scenes in pictures and by extension daily life. Students also learn to make photographs with a sociological lens—a dual focus in undergraduate instruction on the analyzing and making of images anchors an "exhilarating apprenticeship" for visual sociologists (Grady 2001, 118). These assignments enhance students' sociological imagination and immerse them in the research processes of collecting and analyzing data, formulating questions, and writing.

In both sections of this chapter I detail the process and highlight the engagement and discoveries I see in my students' images and writings. My classes are as much about learning to see and think as they are about learning specific disciplinary content. The ideas I share reflect my wide-ranging goals as an educator—sharpening students' observational skills, improving their interest and skills in writing, inspiring creativity, enhancing critical thinking and self-reflection, and expanding visual literacy.

NEW DIRECTIONS FOR TEACHING AND LEARNING • DOI: 10.1002/tl

Photography and Self-Expression

The self/other portrait assignment encompasses many of the core principles of LTP—it involves peer collaboration, looking at life stories from multiple perspectives and negotiating representation dilemmas, putting the self in a social context, communicating with the language of images, studying the interplay between words and images, and "curating" a final piece. Working with a partner, each student creates two portraits—a self-portrait and an other-self portrait—both of which weave together words and images. The making of each portrait starts with writing, which leads to dialogue and collaborative picture making, which then inspires more writing.

Self-Portraits.   I first ask students to jot down on a Post-it an object of special importance. The Post-its are then passed around the room, and each student adds a question about the object listed. Sarah's object, "a small piece of glass surrounded by wire, like an ornament/suncatcher," prompted questions like "Did you make it yourself?"; "Where did you display it?"; "What do you think of when you look at it?"; and "Who else knows about its significance to you?" Urged on by classmates' questions, students write in a free, informal style about their object and anything else that comes to mind. Partners then share their "free-writes" and plan pictures that relate to key words or phrases in the writing. Unlike a self-portrait that chronicles one's day or captures a personality trait, these free-writes often take the photography in unexpected directions, leading students to represent symbolically memories, feelings, or dreams.

Sarah's Self-Portrait.   We see Sarah's shadowy reflection in the dimly lit background of her portrait. She's holding a camera, photographing a dangling piece of glass—a gift, we learn, from a young friend who has since died. Her deeply personal writing begins "at first I thought this object was too specific to be a really good self-portrait. But I recognize now that it shows my love for writing, the value I place on writing, and more. It's actually the most appropriate object for a self-portrait I own." In the absence of a photographic memento, the glass is a reminder of their friendship; it symbolizes her passion for writing, something that once connected the two friends, and her devotion to keep writing, in some ways for the friend she lost.

David's Self-Portrait.   In a more whimsical self-portrait titled "Look Ma, No Hands" (Figure 3.1), David hangs upside down in a tree, wearing the toe shoes he listed as an important object. He writes "As I hang from this low-lying branch, I can't help but think, what would happen if I would fall? ... " He reminisces about younger and carefree days when he could leave it to his mother to worry about his precarious footing on high up branches. Being outdoors is now his fallback strategy for escaping the pressures of college and getting into medical school.

In both of these examples, the skillful combination of words and images complicates the portraits. The words enhance the image's meaning and

Figure 3.1. David's Self-Portrait

vice versa, which is always a goal in LTP. I happened to be walking around campus when I spotted someone hanging from a Magnolia tree in the distance. As I got closer and realized it was David and his partner making portraits, I delighted in the way they embraced the assignment. Yet, I would have missed the layered meaning of his smiling face without his words to guide my interpretation.

Other-Self Portraits.   Partners continue to learn about one another when making other-self portraits, a process that again begins with writing questions. This time their questions focus not on concrete objects but on the far-reaching notion of social identity. Students draw connections between individuals and history, culture, community, language, the body, and so on. To facilitate reflection on the ways social identities such as gender and race/ethnicity or nationality shape experiences, I suggest open-ended questions such as "When did you first become aware of your race/ethnicity and what do you remember about that moment?" or "Where do you feel most safe/unsafe?" "What stereotypes related to your social identities most offend you? Which ones do you identity with?" Students compose four or five questions designed specifically for their partner and in exchange respond in writing to the questions supplied by their partner. Rather than making a second *self*-portrait about their own responses, I challenge students to portray their partners, using their partner's written material as a guide.

David's Other-Self Portrait, Posing as Dominique.   Students literally stand in for their partner—soliciting advice from each other as much or as little as they choose. In other words, in his other-self portrait David, a Midwestern Chinese American, poses as Dominique, a white Southerner with a French-Canadian father. With a set of two photos David embodies and resists the stereotypes of white Southern femininity that Dominique wrote of in response to his questions. In one photograph David descends a wide staircase in an old home. With his tuxedo and warm smile, he looks to be making an appearance for a first date or long-anticipated prom. In his second image he stands at a stove and with a serious expression he swings a frying pan behind his head, as though determined to smash the other pots or send them flying across the room. Through the imagined perspective of Dominique, he writes about Southern belles, old school charm, domestic wives, and keeping the house tidy and the husband happy with a warm dinner on the stove awaiting him.

The other-self assignment is a variation of the Black Self/White Self LTP project my colleagues and I have described in detail (Ewald, Hyde, and Lord 2011) in which young students portray imagined "other" selves with a racial identity other than their own. Here, rather than portraying an imaginary self, I want my students to portray a real person—their classmate. Again the effectiveness of their portraits hinges on the combination of words and images. To inspire students' experimentation with a question/answer format and shifting perspectives/voices, I share Denise Levertov's poem "What Were They Like?" (Levertov 2013). An outsider asks six questions about "the people of Viet Nam" and another foreigner's chilling responses recount the war's devastation on the people's light hearts and rice paddies, ornaments and songs.

My students' frank questions imply a willingness to trust one another, something likely fostered by our small class size, the experience of working together on creative projects with children, and their growing accustomed to reflective writing during each class meeting. Many students wrote poems, and as in Levertov's, their questions provoke elaborate and intimate, sometimes poignant or painful, answers. In her other-self photograph Sarah's face is buried in a book, behind a tall stack of books (Figure 3.2). Just as the image's nine books suggest extensive interests and knowledge, Sarah's poem, which poses six questions that are followed by imagined answers, paints Hanna as multifaceted and evolving.

Sarah's Other-Self Portrait, Posing as Hanna.
What was she like?

1. Where did culture fit, caught between East Coast uptight and a color-blocked calendar?

NEW DIRECTIONS FOR TEACHING AND LEARNING • DOI: 10.1002/tl

Figure 3.2. Sarah's Other-Self Portrait

2. What was her childhood for her, the other side of the country, the other side of the world?
3. Where was she rooted, where did the tree of her stretch?
4. How did she like to be labeled, written, spoken of?
5. Where did she turn for comfort?
6. Was she black enough?

Answers

1. Find it where you can, seek it out, search for it with no map, but the scents and sounds of home, drawing you back, pulling you in. Feel your parents' language on your lips.
2. Fresh California fruit on Saturday morning and seven good books, devouring both.
3. Ethiopia: ancient and unique.
   African-American is an umbrella the size of a continent. You stake your history in the specificity of Ethiopia.
4. Ethiopian-American as a marker of culture, black as a marker of race—the first a way to see inside you, the second a way to stretch your features.
5. Your mother when you were young, a child, close to her everyday; now, older and different, your father.

Figure 3.3. Leilani's Other-Self Portrait

6. No. Not for some here. But how much does it matter? You are typical for an Ethiopian-American girl, rejecting nothing, limiting nothing. Surrounded by people who comprehend, never fail to accept.

This assignment requires introspection and builds empathy as students depict and encounter themselves in their classmates' portrayals. Students took risks in dealing with sensitive material, whether or not they delved explicitly into themes of culture, race, and gender. In her other-self portrait (Figure 3.3), Leilani sits facing an empty chair that was once occupied by her partner's father, who has recently died. Leilani's writing imagines a poignant dialogue where a father responds with warmth, humor, and reassurance to his daughter's difficult questions.

The making of other-self portraits certainly challenges students. In separate papers that reflected on the project, some wrote about their discomfort with portraying their peers. As the collaborations unfold, students remain respectful and even cautious with one another. I hope the inevitable incompleteness of their portraits provokes a nuanced awareness of the immense challenge journalists, documentarians, and social scientists routinely confront when representing individuals and communities.

Photography and Sociological Inquiry

Reading photographs is an essential component of the above LTP activities as well as the sociology assignments described next. As a preliminary

NEW DIRECTIONS FOR TEACHING AND LEARNING • DOI: 10.1002/tl

exercise in classes involving photo-based research, I ask students to identify sociological themes and questions suggested by photographs' concrete
details. To make the exercise more captivating, we examine photos students
have made for a practice shooting assignment where the only guideline is to
take 20 pictures in four settings. I select one photo from each student's work
to introduce this process of reading photos with a sociological lens. We look
at athletic fields, dorm room decorations, messy closets, tailgate parties, library stacks, dumpsters, landscapes, bus stops, and food. We contemplate
the ideas, rules, or habits underneath the everyday scenes pictured. Looking at a photo of a Duke women's soccer match, we might ask—For what
reasons do people play sports? Why are certain sports gender-segregated?
What draws in spectators? Where do the resources for the field, stands,
lights, and equipment come from? Who maintains the field and the stands?
What role do athletics play in higher education? I encourage multiple interpretations, acknowledge that assumptions are unavoidable, and stress that
although photographs reveal only part of the story, they raise questions that
can guide further investigation of countless topics.

Sociological Analysis of Family Photographs. Students write
about a family photograph by placing their intimate object within a broader
cultural, historical, and sociological context. I suggest as examples the
memorable essays in Deborah Willis's edited volume *Picturing Us: African
American Identity in Photography* (Willis 1996). Students write eloquently
about the distinctive stories spiraling out from archetypal photos of family
reunions and vacations, weddings and Christmas mornings, or rare moments such as a grandfather's Olympic race. They question the truthfulness
of images and the constructed meanings of "family," for example, in the context of a graduation shot where a father's pride belies his routine absence.
Students might contemplate a snapshot of a family that has since split up, a
smiling senior portrait now associated with a painful time of coming out, or
a picture of a never-met great-grandfather studying the *Bible*. They consider
how the same photo evokes different emotions, memories, and truths from
different views.

As in the example that follows, students imagine how personal pictures
shape and reflect knowledge, feelings, and worldviews. The assignment led
Sally to a box of photographs she'd never seen and a shocking discovery
that her Chinese parents participated in DC protests against the Tiananmen
Square Massacre:

> ... What I see shapes how I feel about my dad and not the other way around.
> My existing perception of my dad being a pacifist, a generally apathetic per-
> son was completely shattered by these images ... I have always seen him as
> very much a "Dad" figure—driving my brother and me to piano lessons,
> swim meets, and soccer games, and cooking for us at home, mowing the
> lawn, etc.... I have seen little evidence of his involvement in the public
> sphere ... My response ... was a mixture of surprise and pride ... My dad has

always taught us to love China, and in the past, there were times that I thought he couldn't separate the government from the country, and this frustrated me. Now, though, I realize that indeed he could...stand up and protest the government response even while retaining a deep-seated love for his native land...[My parents were] originally planning on returning to China after graduate school, but after the Tiananmen massacre, they decided to stay in the United States. What was initially a study abroad experience for them turned into full-fledged immigration without advance planning, and I'm sure that must have been a very difficult point in their lives...

Sally lists dozens of questions regarding the context and implications of the photograph:

...How did they decide to participate?...Did participation in the protests affect any other parts of my parents' lives?...What are my parents' views now? Would they ever do it again?...What were the responses of other American citizens to the Tiananmen massacre? Were Chinese students the only ones who protested...how were they portrayed in the media? ...Why is the Tiananmen massacre still such a sensitive topic today?...

I hope the assignment piques students' curiosity and urges them to dig deeper. Reading this nearly 2000-word essay, I see how students' personal connection to photographs inspires their writing and how closely inspecting photographs' details helps students frame written arguments. In Sally's essay we see how the serious expression captured on a father's face engenders a complex rethinking of thousands of smiles and shared moments. She eloquently connects personal and global histories, showing how a single image can (re)shape family understanding and chronicle a history her parents prudently kept hidden since China forbade any mention of Tiananmen.

Using the Camera as a Research Tool.   I introduce students to taking pictures in the field with the shooting scripts method, which uses a list of straightforward questions or topics to guide photography. We first study the Farm Security Administration's ambitious script for capturing the essence of American life during the New Deal Era (Garver 1968). Charles Suchar's article "Grounding Visual Sociology in Shooting Scripts" provides another useful guide for how to organize, code, and analyze photographic data (Suchar 1997). I provide students with a shooting script that borrows directly from the above works and connects with other readings, such as Douglas Harper's classic visual ethnography about a mechanic and his small shop (Harper 1987). Students investigate two local independent establishments where the employees work with their hands, using these questions:

1. *How do the employees use their hands in their line of work? What tasks do the employees perform with their hands?*
2. *What do the shops sell or what services do they provide?*

NEW DIRECTIONS FOR TEACHING AND LEARNING • DOI: 10.1002/tl

3. *Who are the customers or clients served by these establishments?*
4. *Who works, owns, or manages these establishments?*

With the focus on hands, students cannot get by with pictures of storefronts taken from a distance. They must engage their subjects in conversations and get close to gather specific visual information. Working alone or in pairs, my students have chosen such sites as floral, tattoo, and bicycle shops, nail and beauty salons, barbershops, and jazz lounges. The assignment involves taking at least 20 pictures in two sites, writing field notes about each site, coding the entire set of pictures, and conducting a preliminary analysis. Coding pictures one at a time, students realize that even didactic pictures are full of information they may not have noticed when shooting. Each photo answers one or more script question while eliciting many other questions. I hope students become more interested in research with this opportunity to study fascinating (even at times beautiful and artistic) visual data. In the tattoo shop, the blue razor, boxes of needles, black latex gloves, reclining chairs, and bookmarked design pages on a laptop all provide information about the nature of work, while the huge tattoo (of a tattoo artist at work) on the side of a male employee's torso gives clues about how he identifies with his job. The small stickers on shelves suggest political leanings and the gendering of space. The absence of uniforms, the color, condition and design on an employee's T-shirt, a workstation's Buddha sculpture, the floor's surface, and the lighting fixtures provide clues about occupational culture, marketing strategies, and customer base.

In written analyses, students identify three patterns that emerged during coding, discuss patterns within patterns, and consider the sociological relevance of the patterns detected. They develop a revised shooting script and explain how it builds on the initial set of pictures and promises to expand one's understanding of the site and relevant social themes. Navigating one's role as a photographer/researcher contextualizes theoretical discussions regarding power dynamics in the practice of photography. While my classes are not about research methods per se, students gain valuable first-hand research experience as they learn how to use the camera to address specific questions, organize data, label and code photos, integrate inductive and deductive research, identify patterns, refine research questions, and consider which types of questions can/cannot be answered through photography.

The shooting scripts exercise might be a one-off assignment in my Sociology through Photography class or the basis for a semester-long project, as in my course Visual Research and the American Dream, where students have studied food banks, homeless shelters and thrift stores, racial segregation among students, campus political involvement during an election season, collegiate athletics, Latino immigration in Durham, or gentrification in the downtown area. At each stage of their ongoing fieldwork, students revise their shooting script and refine their topic. Experimenting with how

NEW DIRECTIONS FOR TEACHING AND LEARNING • DOI: 10.1002/tl

Figure 3.4. Scene from Hannah's Family's Tobacco Farm

to represent and communicate an idea visually requires students to apply their knowledge. They eventually design a final essay incorporating text and about 20 images. Students consider how the meaning or impact of their photos changes through the process of editing and sequencing. They explore the relationship between words and images, and whether the presence of words (titles, captions, excerpts from interviews or field notes) alters the meaning of an image.

After taking both classes mentioned above, Hannah completed a year-long study of her family's Burley tobacco farm (Figures 3.4 and 3.5). Interested in the cultural and economic reasons for her family's persistence in a precarious industry, she shot thousands of images picturing roughly calloused hands, tractor repairs, piles of paper and Post-it notes around a computer, family meals, red faces squinting in the sun, storm clouds over an open field, and worry on her brother's face and in her parents' gestures. These photographs grounded all her fieldwork—fieldnotes, interviews, and written reflections (by her family members as well).

Her outstanding documentary photography and sociological analysis in this intensely personal project connect back to the student-centered philosophy of LTP activities that allows students to link assigned material to their own lives, make choices about the topics they write about and study, and recognize their own experiences as rich and legitimate material for study. Her work is an example of how photography can engross students in their research process—helping them develop their understanding of a topic in stages as they move between data collection and analysis, always going deeper.

NEW DIRECTIONS FOR TEACHING AND LEARNING • DOI: 10.1002/tl

Figure 3.5. Scene from Hannah's Family's Tobacco Farm

References

Ewald, W., K. Hyde, and L. Lord. 2011. *Literacy and Justice through Photography: A Class-room Guide*. New York, NY: Teachers College Press.

Ewald, W., and A. Lightfoot. 2001. *I Wanna Take Me a Picture: Teaching Photography and Writing to Children*. Boston, MA: Beacon Press.

Garver, T. H. 1968. *Just before the War; Urban America from 1935 to 1941 as Seen by Photographers of the Farm Security Administration. With an Introduction by Thomas H. Garver, and Prefatory Notes by Arthur Rothstein, John Vachon, and Roy Stryker*. New York, NY: October House.

Grady, J. 2001. "Becoming a Visual Sociologist." *Sociological Imagination* 38 (1/2): 83–119.

Harper, D. 1987. *Working Knowledge: Skill and Community in a Small Shop*. Chicago, IL: University of Chicago Press.

Hyde, K. 2005. "Portraits and Collaborations: A Reflection on the Work of Wendy Ewald." *Visual Studies* 20 (2): 171–189.

Levertov, D. 2013. *The Collected Poems of Denise Levertov*. New York, NY: New Directions.

Suchar, C. 1997. "Grounding Visual Sociology Research in Shooting Scripts." *Qualitative Sociology* 20 (1): 33–55.

Turkle, S. 2011. *Alone Together: Why We Expect More from Technology and Less from Each Other*. New York, NY: Basic Books.

Willis, D., ed. 1996. *Picturing Us: African American Identity in Photography*. New York, NY: The New Press.

KATHERINE HYDE *is the director of Literacy Through Photography, a program based at the Center for Documentary Studies at Duke University.*

This chapter describes three examples of using illusions to teach visual perception. The illusions present ways for students to change their perspective regarding how their eyes work and also offer opportunities to question assumptions regarding their approach to knowledge.

Seeing Is the Hardest Thing to See: Using Illusions to Teach Visual Perception

Cedar Riener

Close your eyes for a few seconds.

Now that you have opened them, gaze around the room. Look out the window. This effortless, instantaneous action seems perhaps the simplest thing a person can do. We can easily see this assumption of simplicity in the language we use to describe looking: it seems perfectly natural to remind someone to "just look," or even to begin this sentence with "we can easily see." In my classes on visual perception, I urge my students to take a closer look at something that rarely gets a closer look, the act of seeing itself. In order to do so, I use visual illusions as a pedagogical tool to effect a transformation, not in how students see the world, but how they understand their own process of perception. They realize this shift by becoming aware of, questioning, and then rejecting three fundamental assumptions about vision. I have found that an effective way to bring about this transformation is not simply through reading and study, but by directly experiencing mind-blowing visual illusions. I begin by framing these three assumptions in terms of the psychology of visual perception, but student assumptions about seeing often overlap with assumptions about knowledge, a topic that every instructor in higher education must take into account. Illusions can not only remind students how these assumptions mislead them on their understanding of visual perception but can also be used as a launching point for discussions about the nature of knowledge in any discipline.

The first assumption is that vision is simple. Many students enter college courses unaware of the complexity of the subject they are about to study. For example, courses in sociology, philosophy, and political science ask students to see layers and spectra where they might have previously only seen black and white, good and bad, and right and wrong. Other

New Directions for Teaching and Learning, no. 141, Spring 2015 © 2015 Wiley Periodicals, Inc.
Published online in Wiley Online Library (wileyonlinelibrary.com) • DOI: 10.1002/tl.20121

disciplines may find the visual perception exercises that follow interesting ways to get students to appreciate that even that which seems the most simple—seeing—is in fact quite complex. A straightforward historical fact or a brief poem may hide layers of complexity. An illusion can serve as an invitation to look closer at what seems simple and obvious, a common beginning in many college courses.

The second assumption is that vision is immediate, rather than the result of a process. The instantaneous nature of vision is another assumption that applies to multiple disciplines. Attention to the product of vision (our perception of the world itself) can help students forget that perception is a process with many steps. This "unbundling" of the immediate is another common student learning goal in other disciplines. For example, many beginning writers write as they speak (instantaneously), unable to appreciate the process that crafting good prose requires. In other areas of science, many students mistakenly believe in a solitary, "Eureka!" narrative of scientific discovery, instead of the long, gradual, collaborative process that is far more typical.

Finally, many students enter college courses with an epistemology of naïve realism. But for a few trivial exceptions, the world is as it appears. But this is not true. We don't merely sense the real world, but we perceive a human world. Through our sensitivity to certain kinds of light energy, and our understanding of objects that matter to us, we don't passively record an objective reality; we actively create our own subjective reality. Most of this reality we see is agreed upon and shared with every human being, but that doesn't make it any less dependent on the viewer. The subjective nature of perception also applies to history, where to develop an understanding of historiography, students need to first recognize that different observers can have different perspectives on—and interpretations of—the same event.

Any class on visual perception must therefore begin by helping students become aware of a process so obvious that most don't even imagine it being included in a psychology class: seeing the world. How then do I help students to find complexity in the act of seeing a table? How do I help them see the process in perceiving a grid of black squares? How do I get them to understand that what seems black and white is quite often shades of gray? Rather than explaining the transformative nature of education to my students, I find the best way to change students' perspectives is to confound them with unique perceptual experiences that introduce a bit of doubt and confusion into their understanding of visual perception. Visual illusions offer an excellent way to turn a mirror on our own process of perception and be surprised at what we see. In this chapter, I will describe three case studies of using illusory images to teach content in visual perception. However, I believe that each of these demonstrations can also serve pedagogical purposes in courses in other fields. Questioning what we once took for granted is often a central goal of most of higher education, and these illusions can serve as an inspiration for opening eyes, and minds, in other disciplines as

NEW DIRECTIONS FOR TEACHING AND LEARNING • DOI: 10.1002/tl

Figure 4.1. Hermann Grid

well. While students may begin college courses expecting simply to add to their knowledge and skills, college instructors know that education is not merely the filling of a bucket. For this reason, these brief exercises in understanding vision can serve as an inspiration for adopting a different model of learning. Education is not merely accumulation, but learning to see the world differently.

Count the Black Dots

The Hermann grid is a simple illusion, which nonetheless illustrates the great complexity of our visual system. It is composed of a grid of black squares (see Figure 4.1). But when one focuses on the middle, it appears that toward the sides, the white spaces between the black squares have blurry black dots. I title the image "Count the black dots," which leads to students chuckling and looking confused as they experience their eyes "chasing" the dots away as they move their eyes around the image to try to focus on them.

   This illusion has several general lessons for beginning students of perception, as well as several specific ones. The first is the lesson alluded to in the introduction to this chapter: Our experience of perception is that it is simple, instantaneous, and accurate, but this image shows that the world is not what it seems. Second, and related, an image is not something that is passively received, but something that is constructed or built. In this case, the viewer has the experience of changing the image by moving one's eyes around it, and this experience reinforces a core theme of the course. The world that we see is not simply an accurate copy of the real world, but a product of a visual system that takes information from the light and combines that information with assumptions, guesses, and other cues not apparent in the light. Third, what we see when we are looking directly at something is different from something just a few inches away. While the world may all seem to be equally in focus, this illusion illustrates that whatever is

NEW DIRECTIONS FOR TEACHING AND LEARNING • DOI: 10.1002/tl

in our peripheral vision is not just more blurry, but qualitatively different from that on which we are focused.

I find this an excellent illusion to present on the very first day, deceptive in its simplicity, but profound in its insights for the process of perception. In later sections, I again use this illusion to illustrate more advanced perceptual concepts. I will explain one of them below, but it requires a little bit of background.

One of the goals of the course is to understand how our brains take the information from the light and produce our amazing and rich visual experience. To understand the mechanism of this process, we begin with the physics of light, then move to biology of the eye and brain, and finally to our psychological experience of sight. We begin with the light from the sun reflecting off surfaces in the world. That light enters our eye through the pupil, and hits the retina, or the back of our eye. The retina contains our photoreceptors, the specialized neurons (yes, photoreceptors are neurons, humans have "brains" in their eyes) that take in light and translate it into electrochemical brain signals. The photoreceptors therefore send their brain signals to other neurons, which send their signals to other neurons, and so on. These other neurons are organized into layers that take information from one layer, process it by virtue of how they are "wired" together, and send it along to the next set of neurons. The upshot of all these neurons sending messages to one another is that our brain takes the raw light bouncing off of surfaces and entering our eyes and translates this light into your friend waving at you from across the room, or the soccer ball being blasted right at you, or that car taking a left turn up ahead.

How do we understand how the wiring of neurons relates to the experience they provide? One critical piece of this mapping between nerve structure and visual experience is the concept of a neuron's receptive field. A receptive field is the pattern of light on the retina that corresponds to the highest level of activity for a given neuron. In other words, there is a pattern of light that each neuron involved in vision "prefers." For example, a photoreceptor's (the neurons located directly on the retina) receptive field is easy to please: when a light hits that photoreceptor, it gets happy. Its receptive field is therefore a dot of light at its location on the retina. But the neurons further along in the chain (those that get their information from many photoreceptors) have more complicated patterns of light that activate them more strongly; their receptive fields are more like maps than points. Some neurons prefer a donut shape of light; some prefer an edge of light next to darkness.

Now that we understand what a receptive field is, we can understand a bit more about the Hermann grid. The traditional explanation for the Hermann grid is that we see the black dots due to differences between the receptive fields of central and peripheral cells in the retina (neurons several layers further along in the chain of communication than the photoreceptors). The cells in the periphery (where the black dots appear) are

Figure 4.2. Adelson Checkerboard

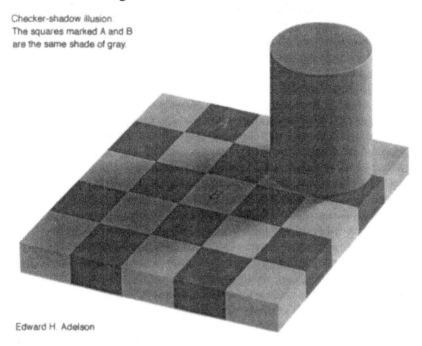

"inhibited" (their activity is dampened) by the adjacent white areas between the black squares. Larger receptive fields are more sensitive to what is called lateral inhibition, where an area of lightness (by activating photoreceptors) causes an increased contrast (darkness) in the area of space directly adjacent (by inhibiting cells further down the chain of communication). The Hermann grid, this simple grid of black squares, then becomes a way of explaining how the patterns of light in the world become translated into biological messages, which then result in psychological experiences. From apparent simplicity to amazing complexity, this is a great message to begin any course.

This Is Not a Checkerboard

The next illusion is called the Adelson checkerboard (Figure 4.2). A checkerboard with a green cylinder is depicted. Two squares, A and B, are labeled. While they appear to be different shades of gray, they are in fact identical. What lesson does this illusion offer us?

While students may not feel as if their mind is performing a calculation to arrive at their perception of the colors of the checkerboard, this illusion reminds them that perception is a process. Instead of taking in the grays of squares A and B and immediately seeing the color, our visual system takes into account the entire picture in *deciding* which gray is darker. In this case, the green cylinder, and indeed the shading of the entire checkerboard, contributes to our process of judging the color of square B.

How do our eyes calculate the brightness of surfaces? The intensity of light that gets into our eye depends both on how much light is shining on a surface and how reflective that surface is. The problem is that we can't recover the individual elements—the reflectiveness of the surface and the strength of the light shining on it—only given the single amount of light that gets into our eye. The same amount of light can enter an eye by a bright light shining on a dark surface as a dim light shining on a bright surface. I use this illusion to introduce a bit of necessary jargon. The amount of light that hits a surface is called illumination. How much light a surface tends to bounce off is called reflectance. And the amount of light that finally gets into one's eye from that surface is called luminance. So, a given level of luminance is necessarily a combination of reflectance and illumination.

Applying this to the Adelson checkerboard, square B seems to be in shadow (low illumination) and yet has medium luminance, so we judge that it must be reflective (light gray paint). Square A, on the other hand, seems to be in bright light (high illumination) and yet has the same luminance as B, so we judge that it must have low reflectance (dark gray paint). Our visual system makes all of these "decisions" without any awareness on our part. Of course there is a shadow, since there is a cylinder there. But there is no cylinder (again, I rub my hand over the green shape), only a green shape here, that has darker green on one side than the other.

In this illusion, we can also experience the change in perception when we cover up the rest of the figure. When a shape covers up the cylinder and the rest of the checkerboard, the two squares appear identical. Adding and removing this shape show how our visual system persists in seeing the squares as different, even though we know that they are the same. Students sometimes ask why this is, and whether we can teach our eyes to see this the "correct" way? The answer is that we have already "taught" our eyes to see it exactly the way that we do; we have spent all our time on Earth viewing shadows, teaching our eyes to understand which surfaces are reflective and which surfaces are brightly illuminated. This illusion illustrates the rules that we have learned through extensive experience and training. When objects seem to be the same color, like green, but have some portions darker than others, they are more likely in shadow than painted with a gradient. These rules are highly effective in the real world, but illusions reveal them as educated guesses. These guesses show not only the process of decision making that occurs in the instant of perceiving this image, but also that they are the result of a long process of learning how to see. Such an illusion also makes an interesting analogy to language comprehension and literature. The process of reading a sentence does not merely occur in the moment of reading that sentence, but the years of learning to read, the many experiences one has had with reading those particular words.

NEW DIRECTIONS FOR TEACHING AND LEARNING • DOI: 10.1002/tl

Figure 4.3. Shepard Tables

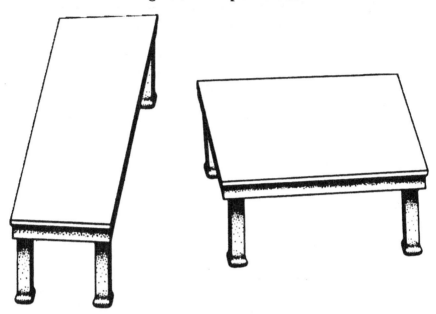

Tabletops

The final illusion is called the Shepard tables, invented by Roger Shepard (1990). Two tables are shown (see Figure 4.3). The question is, "Which table has the longer tabletop?" The answer is that each tabletop has exactly the same shape. The one on the right is merely a rotated version of the one on the left. In class, I chose to demonstrate this by exiting "presenter mode" in PowerPoint and actually selecting the shape of the tabletop on the left, rotating it, then moving it over to the table on the right. It fits perfectly, provoking a chorus of "ooohs" and "aaaaahs" and "no waaaaaays!"

What are the lessons for this illusion? First, the world is not as it seems. In particular, this illusion highlights the difference between the flatness of the image on the eyes (or on the paper) and our perception of a three-dimensional world. In this case, because our visual system is so accustomed to taking flat images from our eyes and translating them into the three-dimensional world, we cannot see the tables as simply flat images. The shapes themselves are flat (I walk up to the projector screen and run my hand over them at this point), but we can't see them as flat. Why? Because with even the mere hint of three-dimensionality, in this case the legs and the shading on the legs, our eyes see this image as a depiction of a three-dimensional scene, not as a flat image on paper.

Such a reaction evokes what perceptual psychologist James Gibson has called the "dual awareness" of pictures. When we view pictures, we can be aware of both the object being depicted and the artistic elements of the picture itself. However, even when we can have a dual awareness, the default of our perceptual system is to see "through" the flat depiction straight into the three-dimensional world.

The second more specific lesson for this illusion is that shape and orientation are not specified by the retinal image. Think of a shape on the retina as similar to a shadow. A shadow of a square could be a square held perpendicular between the light and the screen, or it could be a trapezoid held at an angle. In the image of the Shepard tables, our visual system judges both the shapes and the orientations at the same time, seeing them as different shapes at different orientations, when in fact they are both flat on the paper and of the same shape.

Concluding Thoughts

In closing, I believe that each of these case studies shows that studying images through illusions can offer lessons not just for students of visual perception, but for students of many disciplines in higher education.

Illusions show that perception is not simple. Ask students what is the most difficult thing that their brain does, and they might come up with solving difficult puzzles, or playing chess, or feats of memory. But the truth is that watching TV and making sense of the flickering light is anything but simple. The ability to recognize a friend's face from across a crowded room is anything but simple. Just because we aren't aware of something doesn't make it trivial. I can see this being a valuable lesson in history, or art, or even math. These three illusions are each simple to reproduce but reveal the complexity in how we see. As the explanations show, understanding the mechanisms for how we perceive that grid of black dots relies on knowledge of the biological structures of the eye, as well as communication and organization of neurons in the eye.

Illusions show that perception is a process. With the Hermann grid, viewers experience this in real time. But the other illusions also offer the chance to see perception as a process. Rotating the tabletop in the Shepard tables illusion shows how difficult it is to keep track of flat shapes when our visual system cannot stop seeing the world in three dimensions. Covering up the rest of the checkerboard and the green cylinder in the Adelson checkerboard shows how the visual system makes assumptions and decisions ("the light source is on the right side, out of sight, but the green cylinder is blocking it"). While we are unable to slow down this process, we can nonetheless experience what happens when certain steps in the process are misdirected. This is the value of experiencing illusions: they help us become aware of perception as a decision-making process by causing us to experience when our brain makes the wrong decision.

Finally, illusions show us that the world is not as it seems. "Look closer" might be the first message of experiencing a particularly compelling illusion. But quickly following comes a realization that the reality and the looking are not as tightly coupled as we once thought. Illusions make us question what we are seeing, and in doing so, cause us to look closer, not just at the world, but at ourselves.

Reference

Shepard, R. 1990. *Mindsights*. New York, NY: Freeman.

CEDAR RIENER *is a professor of psychology at Randolph–Macon College.*

NEW DIRECTIONS FOR TEACHING AND LEARNING • DOI: 10.1002/tl

This chapter describes the challenges and benefits of working with images in a history classroom. The first part indicates the complexity of helping students use images as historical evidence; the second argues that close readings of images can help students develop their deep attention skills as they question the evidence they see; and the final discusses how work with images can be done in a way that accommodates all students, including those with limited or no sight.

How to Navigate an "Upside-Down" World: Using Images in the History Classroom

Steven S. Volk

In 1615, Felipe Guaman Poma de Ayala sent a 1,189-page "chronicle" to King Philip III of Spain.[1] Its author was born near present-day Ayacucho, Peru, sometime after the 1533 Spanish conquest of the Inca Empire. Heir to a Quechua-speaking, preconquest provincial nobility, Guaman Poma served as translator and assistant to two Spanish priests and a judge. He was one of a handful of bilingual indigenous writers in colonial Peru to author narratives of the Inca and pre-Incaic past and of native life under colonization that attempted to be intelligible to the Spanish while remaining faithful to Andean cultural traditions (Adorno 1986; Wilson 1998). Guaman Poma's *Corónica* [sic] is a stunning work, not only in its critique of Spanish rule, but in its inclusion of nearly 400 full-page narrative drawings by the author.

Teaching Guaman Poma to undergraduates presents a triple challenge. In the first place, the very *foreignness* of his text, with its frequent code switches between Quechua and Spanish and its early modern orthography, supports Carlo Ginzburg's observation that "The more we discover about [past] people's mental universes, the more we should be shocked by the cultural distance that separates us from them" (quoted in Wineburg 2001, 10). Secondly, the *Chronicle* makes us equally aware of the cultural chasm that stood between the author and his targeted audience, Philip III (who, in fact, never read it). Finally, Guaman Poma's beguiling drawings remind us that historians have few conventions for reading images as evidence (Coventry et al. 2006). While they first appear to be "only" textual illustrations, they

New Directions for Teaching and Learning, no. 141, Spring 2015 © 2015 Wiley Periodicals, Inc.
Published online in Wiley Online Library (wileyonlinelibrary.com) • DOI: 10.1002/tl.20122

strongly hint at the presence of a parallel narrative to which viewers must find a point of access.

The challenge of Guaman Poma provides an illustrative case for considering the uses of images in the undergraduate history classroom, which I will develop on three levels. First, I will explore how historians can make meaning with images, specifically how images can be leveraged to help students gain a greater understanding of the cultural gulf that separates present from past. This process is a complex one, but one that has a place in an undergraduate classroom. Above all, faculty need to be aware of the time it takes to prepare students to engage historical images proficiently. As I will suggest, this is time well spent in a history class. Second, I will suggest how image work can be deployed as a strategy to scaffold students' deep attention skills. A growing literature argues that faculty should attend to not just *what* our students know, but *how* they know. Processes that increase contemplation, that "quiet and shift the habitual chatter of the mind to cultivate a capacity for deepened awareness, concentration, and insight," are valuable for our increasingly hyperconnected students (Hart 2004, 28). Finally, I will recount how teaching with images helped me understand the importance of creating a classroom that fostered the learning of every student. To engage the challenge of making meaning with historical images is, at the same time, to be aware that not all students are sighted. Rather than discarding this powerful methodology, we need to consider how to make our pedagogical approaches accessible to all of our students.

Meaning Making and Images in the History Classroom

A tiny group of native writers took on the "impossible" task of narrating their world for the Spanish conquerors (Salomon 1982). When historians assign these accounts, we face the necessity of bringing students into worlds organized on a radically different set of understandings, particularly as regards concepts of time and history. For the Spanish, for example, it was "in time and therefore in history that the great drama of Sin and Redemption, the central axis of all Christian thought ... unfolded"; each event that occurred was singular and unique (Bloch 1953, 5). The Andean past, by contrast, was understood as a cycle in which similar events acted as "renewed sightings of constant points" (Salomon 1982, 11). Similarly, gaining access to that past was predicated on different mechanisms than those we utilize. Bringing students into an awareness of those understandings through Guaman Poma's complex text always seemed to hit a dead end: they saw the Andean past as a "less developed," not a different, world, much like a child is a "less developed" (but familiar) adult. Perhaps by accessing his images we could find a better passage into that remote epistemology.

In "Time to Sow Potatoes and *Ocas*" (Figure 5.1), a man and a woman work in a field, he digging with a foot plough, she inserting a seed potato from a sack on her back. A second woman uses a rake, while the Sun and

Figure 5.1. Time to Sow Potatoes and *Ocas*

Source: Guaman Poma de Ayala (1615/2001, 1175). Copyright © 2001 by The Royal Library—Copenhagen. Reprinted by permission of The Royal Library—Copenhagen.

Moon look down on a mountainous landscape. The image contains captions and inscriptions in Quechua and Spanish, emphasizing the importance of translation to understanding the author's project. This drawing provides abundant evidence for a discussion of gender and work, foodways, or agricultural technology. At this beginning point, however, students' questions are still shaped by their present: Why don't they use animal-drawn ploughs? How important are potatoes to their diet? But how do we move to Guaman Poma's world, understanding both the meanings of his image and *how* it means (Jaffee 2006; Little, Felten, and Berry 2010)?

I ask the students to shift their view upward, to the Sun and the Moon, and our discussion transitions to issues of iconography, to representations whose meanings surpass literal depiction (Sturken and Cartwright 2001). For Andean peoples at the time of the conquest, the Sun and Moon carried a specific cultural, historical, and social meaning that we needed to access. In other words, if our discussion of agricultural technology can take place within a rationalist world of "less" and "more" developed, entering Andean symbolic systems demands that we enter a past that is not only different

Figure 5.2. World Map of the Kingdom of the Indies

Source: Guaman Poma de Ayala (1615/2001, 1001). Copyright © 2001 by The Royal Library—Copenhagen. Reprinted by permission of The Royal Library—Copenhagen.

from our own, but every bit as logical conceptually. By working through Guaman Poma's images, students begin to appreciate the radical foreignness of this past in a way that the text alone could not convey. Working with the chronicler's illustrations, students become aware of the "richly problematic" process by which historians gain access to the past (Amin 1995).

To dig more deeply into that past, students explore Guaman Poma's "Mapamundi" ("World Map," Figure 5.2). Those who have worked with medieval maps are familiar with the idea that cartography is a "moralized geography" that discloses more about political, religious, or social power than about actual geographic coordinates (Schulz 1978). Our challenge, therefore, becomes how to "make maps 'speak' about the social worlds of the past" (Harley 1988, 281), for when the students look at Guaman Poma's map, they are looking at that past. Guaman Poma's attempt at "translation" in his cartography is immediately evident in the grid he has superimposed on his Andean world, a pattern students typically read as familiar markings of longitude and latitude. But the diagonal lines that cross at the center of the map hint at an utterly different ordering concept (Adorno 1986).

The diagonals, they learn, are an important element of Andean epistemology; they divide space into upper and lower, and right and left fields, and mark a hierarchy of preference, opposition, and complimentarity. The map discloses relations of superiority (*hanan*) and subordination (*hurin*)

NEW DIRECTIONS FOR TEACHING AND LEARNING • DOI: 10.1002/tl

that existed among the four ethnic groups (*collas*) of Cuzco, the center of the Inca Empire, as well as masculine and feminine domains and genealogical schema associated with the Sun and Moon (Adorno 1986; Silverblatt 1987). The students consider this fundamental organizing system further by closely examining a drawing by another native author, reproduced from an image said to have existed in the Coricancha, the Inca's paramount temple in Cuzco (Adorno 1986). In this drawing, Viracocha, the creator god of Andean peoples, occupies the central diagonal, the point of greatest power and authority, dividing the conceptual space between the Sun and Moon, male and female, and sea and earth.

It is almost always at this point that the proverbial penny drops. They do not fully understand Guaman Poma's world—that would take much more study, and, indeed, is not my objective. But they do *see* that people in that world understood themselves and their surroundings in a completely different way than they do. They can appreciate that what is so clear in their own symbolic system—that power rests on a vertical scale, where "up" is more powerful and "down" less—did not work the same for Guaman Poma. Not only does this allow them some access to his other images, but the visual meaning draws them closer to Guaman Poma's harrowing message that under Spanish colonialism, he was living in "*un mundo al-rreués*" (an upside-down world) (Guaman Poma de Ayala 1615/2001, 222). They not only see his meaning, they can feel his anguish.

If images allow students to appreciate that the conceptual world they are trying to enter is quite distant from their own, putting text and images side by side can bring students closer to a "historically contextualized seeing of the visual evidence" (Jaffee 2006, 1382). By counterposing Guaman Poma's text and images, I provide a way for students to appreciate the shadow of resistance he offers to colonial rule. On the *Chronicle's* title page (Figure 5.3), the author has drawn an image of what appears to be native acquiescence to colonial rule. Three crests occupy the central space: in descending order that of the Papacy, the Spanish monarchy, and Guaman Poma himself (*guaman* means "falcon" in Quechua; *poma*, "lion"). The author kneels in supplication to both Church and, in the top left, "su magistad," Philip III. Yet an Andean reading disrupts this meaning. The central space (the crossing of the diagonals) is emptied of the figure of the Spanish king who, instead, is removed to the upper left, to the position of "Collasuyo," the *second* subdivision of the empire and, hence, a symbolic rebuff (Adorno 1986).

Guaman Poma restores the proper (Andean) order in his drawing of the "The Rich Imperial Town of Potosí" (Figure 5.4). In his narrative of Potosí, home to the world's richest silver mine at the time, the chronicler merged text and image to turn the world right side up again. Guaman Poma relocates the figure of the Inca back to the center of the crossed diagonals where he was sustained by the kings of the four imperial "*collas*" who, in turn, supported the royal shield of the Spanish monarchy. The text leaves

Figure 5.3. Title Page: *El Primer Nueva Corónica*

Source: Guaman Poma de Ayala (1615/2001, title page). Copyright © 2001 by The Royal Library—Copenhagen. Reprinted by permission of The Royal Library—Copenhagen.

little to doubt: "Because of [the Potosí] mine, Castile is Castile, Rome is Rome, the pope is pope, and the [Spanish] king is monarch of the world" (Guaman Poma de Ayala 1615/2001, 1065). The Andes sustained the Spanish empire, not the other way around.

By learning to read these images, students sharpen their ability to make meanings according to what James Paul Gee calls the "multimodal principle," stressing that "meaning and knowledge are built up through various modalities... not just words" (Gee 2003, quoted in Felten 2008, 60), and that students will be expected to combine textual sources with communications media in the world outside the classroom. The work they must do to access Guaman Poma's "upside-down" world makes evident to the students how radically different from their own was the conceptual framework through which Andeans understood their world.

Images and Pedagogy: Deep Attention

Our students have grown up surrounded by images that, increasingly, they access via an online environment. A study by the Kaiser Family

Figure 5.4. The Rich Imperial Town of Potosí

Source: Guaman Poma de Ayala (1615/2001, 1065). Copyright © 2001 by The Royal Library—
Copenhagen. Reprinted by permission of The Royal Library—Copenhagen.

Foundation found that young people between 8 and 18 (Generation M2)
spend an average of seven-and-a-half hours a day using entertainment media. Given that a considerable amount of that time is spent "media multi-
tasking," researchers calculate that they are packing nearly eleven hours of
media content into the daily time they spend on various devices (Rideout,
Foehr, and Roberts 2010). Scholars are beginning to examine the conse-
quences of these trends for student learning, and have predicted that Generation M2 will be more skilled at tasks requiring hyperattention, but less
adept at those demanding deep attention. The latter is the ability to focus in
a concentrated fashion on a single topic for extended periods while tuning
out competing demands. Hyperattention, in contrast, is the ability to mul-
titask, to switch "focus rapidly among different tasks, preferring multiple
information streams, seeking a high level of stimulation, and having a low
tolerance for boredom" (Hayles 2007, 187).

Two issues take precedence for teachers when considering this research. In the first place, educational practice, particularly in higher

NEW DIRECTIONS FOR TEACHING AND LEARNING • DOI: 10.1002/tl

education, has long equated the benefits and practice of deep attention with learning itself. Depth, Tobin Hart (2004) argues, "implies higher order understanding and application, creativity, problem-solving, and self-reflection. Deep encounters with knowledge and with one another have the potential to transform the learner and the process of learning" (29). At the same time, a growing number of indicators point out that the skills associated with hyperactivity are, in many cases, well suited to what our graduates will need in their future jobs. If both approaches have merit, Katherine Hayles (2007) asks, "How can the considerable benefits of deep attention be cultivated in a generation of students who prefer high levels of stimulation and have low thresholds for boredom?" (195).

As teachers, we determine the tempo of our classrooms. We can craft our pedagogies purposefully both to increase the productive and responsible use of up-tempo hyperconnectivity and to moderate the pace, ensuring students the time needed to reflect upon their learning (Holt 2002). The careful work of unpacking images has been a central element in a pedagogical strategy I employ to enhance deep attention, encouraging students to "look" more closely in order to "see" more purposefully. At times, I take students to our college art museum to work with artifacts and paintings using a pedagogy specifically designed to enhance deep engagement (Volk and Milkova 2012). More often, this is the work of the classroom, as the next example will demonstrate.

Historians have long considered Chile as one of the most democratic countries in Latin America. But on September 11, 1973, the freely elected socialist president, Salvador Allende, was violently overthrown by the military. As part of class discussions of those events, I ask the students to examine photographs taken in the days surrounding the coup, particularly a photograph of General Augusto Pinochet (Figure 5.5), head of the Army, taken by Chas Gerretsen, a Dutch photographer, eight days after the coup.

In the picture, Pinochet sits scowling, arms crossed on his chest, his aides standing behind him. For students familiar with the general's seventeen-year-long dictatorship, the image represents a photographer's dream, the opportunity to capture a subject as he "truly" is. Pinochet the man and Pinochet the image are one and the same: the iconic Latin American dictator. Because photographs are indexical signs, more than other images they are seen as unmediated (Sturken and Cartwright 2001). But, they are not. Correctly reading historical photography requires even more work given that the "truth" of the photograph often derives from knowledge later acquired and inferred backward (Bromwich 2013, 8). By taking the time to deepen the students' engagement with Gerretsen's photograph, we can develop the image for use as historical evidence.

To access the "testimony of images," Peter Burke (2001) advises, "begin by studying the different purposes of their makers" (19). Who made this photograph, I ask? Gerretsen or Pinochet? Gerretsen's camera captured the scene and the photographer developed, printed, and circulated it. But was it

NEW DIRECTIONS FOR TEACHING AND LEARNING • DOI: 10.1002/tl

Figure 5.5. General Augusto Pinochet (Chas Gerretsen, September 19, 1973)

© Chas Gerretsen/Nederlands Fotomuseum.

a chance or staged shot? In the discussion that follows, as students pursue multiple lines of inquiry, they develop a historically contextualized analysis of the photograph that undercuts their original understanding.

Gerretsen's photograph quickly circulated outside of Chile, becoming a sign of the harshness of Chilean military rule. Given the relatively low quality of most newsprint reproductions, viewers saw a man seemingly hiding from the camera behind his dark glasses. High-quality reproductions, however, reveal that Pinochet's shades were only tinted, and we can see his eyes. In fact, he was the only one in the photograph who glared directly at Gerretsen's camera. Not only was Pinochet not hiding, he was performing. But what was he performing and for whom?

At that point I send the students back to their readings where they find that Pinochet, the head of the Army but still relatively unknown, was the last to join the coup plotters. The students return to the photograph, now to suggest that the general was more interested in a Chilean than an international audience. His message? That it would be a mistake for either his military rivals or the Chilean people to take him as weak or indecisive. Pinochet's dominance, proved over a long dictatorship, was far from certain on September 19, 1973.

The lengthy discussion of Gerresten's photograph offered a way for students to work as historians, challenging their initial assumptions and using visual and textual evidence to search for meaning. By slowing down to explore that moment, students used image work to help them develop the deep attention skills that they would later be asked to demonstrate in research assignments.

Images and Universal Design: Bringing Everyone In

About ten years ago, a student who was extraordinarily excited about Latin America signed up for my Latin American history survey, having spent the previous January term in Guatemala. Matthew had very limited vision. He was born with cataracts, developed glaucoma as a baby, and soon lost all vision in his left eye while retaining only partial sight in the right. He could read with the help of a computer and got around campus without a guide dog or cane. I made sure he was assigned a note taker, and that the readings were available far in advance so they could be recorded. It wasn't long after the semester started, however, that his limited eyesight vanished completely. A corneal ulcer in his "good" eye had become infected. As he was sitting in my class, he later wrote, "Suddenly the lights seemed really bright. Then it got really painful. By the end of the hour I could barely see well enough to get myself to Academic Services" (VanFossan 2013, 24). Matthew had become totally blind.

Matthew barely missed a day of class, and I was forced to ponder how to teach a class using visual methodology where one student could not see. I had been teaching history through images for nearly twenty years at that point. Rarely did I lecture without a generous dose of images on the screen. Now I had to rethink my approach. I considered asking a classmate to sit beside Matthew, quietly describing the visuals I put up. But the continual, if hushed, commentary would have made his disability the center of class attention. Only then did it occur to me that I needed to refocus on my learning goals for the class.

Helping students make meanings with images and better use them as historical evidence remained an important goal. What changed was how I made that happen. Rather than have students absorb the visuals individually, now they would describe them out loud to the class. Many of the slides I showed in my lectures were used to establish background or context: paintings of leaders or maps, for example. But, in each lecture, a few images needed to be observed carefully to make their meanings clearer. From that

NEW DIRECTIONS FOR TEACHING AND LEARNING • DOI: 10.1002/tl

point on, having identified those specific slides, I would halt the lecture and ask students to describe what was going on in the image. First one, then additional students would discuss the slide, each adding to its descriptive, and then interpretative, detail. Not only did Matthew not need a personal coach to do this work for him, but the entire class benefited from developing close reading capabilities and Matthew could partake in the discussion of what further context was needed for us to use this image as historical evidence.

The principle of "universal design" holds that education should be conducted in a way that benefits all and disadvantages none, having as its goal the full inclusion of *all* students (Burgstahler 2008). By making work with images a more intentional part of everyone's work, I created a class that focused attention on the skills I wanted all my students, including Matthew, to have and then scaffolded a learning process around them. Everyone gained in the process.

Conclusion

We live in a world of images, and while working with text, now delivered on a variety of platforms, remains essential for our students, negotiating meanings with visual media is an increasingly valuable skill (Thomas, Place, and Hillyard 2008). As I have suggested, using image work in the history classroom can prove to be a significant means of helping students acquire skills that are an essential part of the historian's tool chest. They learn how to evaluate evidence, how to look closely, how to weigh differing interpretations, and how to see change over time. Working with images can help in other ways as well. Many students benefit from multimodal approaches that open different pathways to the past. In answering David Jaffee's (2006) question about what sort of learning goes on when we incorporate visual materials in our history courses, I have found that image and words work contrapuntally, as a kind of text and countertext, that allows students to question the meaning of historical evidence by placing one beside the other.

Visual work, leading toward a goal of greater visual literacy, is also important in providing students with skills that help bridge the classroom and their postgraduate lives (Luke 2003). By developing consistent work with images, we can help students slow down and develop their deep attention skills. And finally, at least in my case, working with images helped me see what had previously been hidden, that our responsibility as teachers is to create an environment of learning in which all can participate.

Note

1. Guaman Poma's (1615/2001) *El primer nueva corónica [sic] y buen gobierno* (*The First New Chronicle and Good Government*) is available as a high-quality facsimile produced by the Royal Library of Denmark at http://www.kb.dk/permalink/2006/poma/info/en/frontpage.htm. The misspelling of *crónica* is from the original edition.

NEW DIRECTIONS FOR TEACHING AND LEARNING • DOI: 10.1002/tl

References

Adorno, R. 1986. *Guaman Poma: Writing and Resistance in Colonial Peru*. Austin, TX: University of Texas Press.

Amin, S. 1995. *Event, Metaphor, Memory: Chauri Chaura, 1922–1992*. Berkeley: University of California Press.

Bloch, M. 1953. *The Historian's Craft*. Translated by P. Putnam. New York, NY: Vintage Books.

Bromwich, D. 2013, August 15. "The Civil War Pictures: True or False?" *New York Review of Books* 60 (13): 8–10.

Burgstahler, S. E. 2008. "Universal Design in Higher Education." In *Universal Design in Higher Education: From Principles to Practice*, edited by S. E. Burgstahler and R. C. Cory, 23–44. Cambridge, MA: Harvard Education Press.

Burke, P. 2001. *Eyewitnessing: The Uses of Images as Historical Evidence*. Ithaca, NY: Cornell University Press.

Coventry, M., P. Felten, D. Jaffee, C. O'Leary, T. Weis, and S. McGowan. 2006. "Ways of Seeing: Evidence and Learning in the History Classroom." *The Journal of American History* 92 (4): 1371–1382.

Felten, P. 2008. "Visual Literacy." *Change* (November/December): 60–63.

Gee, J. P. 2003. *What Video Games Have to Teach Us about Learning and Literacy*. New York, NY: Palgrave Macmillan.

Guaman Poma de Ayala, F. 1615/2001. *El primer nueva corónica [sic] y buen gobierno* [The Guaman Poma Website]. Copenhagen, Denmark: Department of Manuscripts & Rare Books, Digital Research Center of the Royal Library. http://www.kb.dk/permalink/2006/poma/info/en/frontpage.htm.

Harley, J. B. 1988. "Maps, Knowledge, and Power." In *The Iconography of Landscape: Essays on the Symbolic Representation, Design and Use of Past Environments*, edited by D. Cosgrove and S. Daniels, 277–312. New York, NY: Cambridge University Press.

Hart, T. 2004. "Opening the Contemplative Mind in the Classroom." *Journal of Transformative Education* 2 (1): 28–46.

Hayles, N. K. 2007. "Hyper and Deep Attention: The Generational Divide in Cognitive Modes." *Profession* 2007: 187–199. http://engl449_spring2010_01.commons.yale.edu/files/2009/11/hayles.pdf.

Holt, M. 2002. "It's Time to Start the Slow School Movement." *The Phi Delta Kappan* 84: 264–271.

Jaffee, D. 2006. "Thinking Visually as Historians: Incorporating Visual Methods." *The Journal of American History* 92 (4): 1378–1382.

Little, D., P. Felten, and C. Berry. 2010. "Liberal Education in a Visual World." *Liberal Education* 96 (2): 44–49.

Luke, C. 2003. "Pedagogy, Connectivity, Multimodality, and Interdisciplinarity." *Reading Research Quarterly* 38 (3): 397–402.

Rideout, V., U. Foehr, and D. Roberts. 2010. "Generation M2: Media in the Lives of 8- to 18-Year Olds." Kaiser Family Foundation. http://kaiserfamilyfoundation.files.wordpress.com/2013/04/8010.pdf.

Salomon, F. 1982. "Chronicles of the Impossible: Notes on Three Peruvian Indigenous Historians." In *From Oral to Written Expression: Native Andean Chronicles of the Early Colonial Period*, edited by R. Adorno, 9–39. Syracuse, NY: Maxwell School of Citizenship and Public Affairs, Syracuse University.

Schulz, J. 1978. "Jacopo Barbari's View of Venice: Map Making, City Views and Moralized Geography." *Art Bulletin* 60 (3): 425–474.

Silverblatt, I. 1987. *Moon, Sun, and Witches: Gender Ideologies and Class in Inca and Colonial Peru*. Princeton, NJ: Princeton University Press.

Sturken, M., and L. Cartwright. 2001. *Practices of Looking: An Introduction to Visual Culture*. New York, NY: Oxford University Press.

Thomas, E., N. Place, and C. Hillyard. 2008. "Students and Teachers Learning to See: Part I: Using Visual Images in the College Classroom to Promote Students' Capacities and Skills." *College Teaching* 56 (1): 23–27.

VanFossan, M. 2013. *Through Gilly's Eyes. Memoirs of a Guide Dog.* Pittsburgh, PA: Volant Press.

Volk, S. S., and L. Milkova. 2012. "'Crossing the Street' Pedagogy: Using College Art Museums to Leverage Significant Learning Across the Campus." In *A Handbook for Academic Museums: Exhibitions and Education*, edited by S. S. Jandl and M. S. Gold, 88–118. Edinburgh, UK: MuseumsEtc.

Wilson, L. A. 1998. "Survival, Resistance, and Acculturation: Guaman Poma's Use of Costume and Textile Imagery." *Studies in Iconography* 19: 177–210.

Wineburg, S. 2001. *Historical Thinking and Other Unnatural Acts. Charting the Future of the Past*. Philadelphia, PA: Temple University Press.

STEVEN S. VOLK is a professor of history and the director of the Center for Teaching Innovation and Excellence (CTIE) at Oberlin College.

NEW DIRECTIONS FOR TEACHING AND LEARNING • DOI: 10.1002/tl

This chapter describes a pedagogical approach that blends theory and practice in upper-level French film classes, but the objectives, design, and assignments are applicable to many contexts in which instructors might want to engage with visual material. Reading, viewing, writing, lecture, and discussion combine with practical filmmaking workshops in French in the exploration of historical, social, philosophical, and esthetic questions raised by film and video, and students improve language skills as well as expanding their creativity and problem-solving skills.

Teaching Film and Filmmaking in a Second Language

Alison J. Murray Levine

As an associate professor of French at the University of Virginia, I teach French cinema and cultural studies to upper-division undergraduates and graduate students. Over the past couple of years, I have redesigned all of my courses to include a series of filmmaking workshops and creative audiovisual assignments alongside the more traditional reading, writing, lecture, and discussion on which these courses have always been based. I have found that this blend of theory and practice enables students to be more engaged in their learning and to produce higher-quality analytical and creative work. I hope that instructors in any discipline wishing to deepen their students' engagement with visual material find that the discussion sparks ideas for their own courses.

The audiovisual practice I have recently integrated takes different forms depending on the class. But in all cases, students devote some class time to learning how to use cameras, tripods, lights, sound recording equipment, and editing software; they submit some assignments as digital videos, and they create digital films as part of their final project. All of this work is done in French. This chapter explains my objectives as well as some guidelines for implementation and an overview of the results I have observed with my students.

This project reaches beyond the specific disciplines of film studies and second language courses in several important ways. First, the blended theory-practice model, in which students engage in practical activities that

NEW DIRECTIONS FOR TEACHING AND LEARNING, no. 141, Spring 2015 © 2015 Wiley Periodicals, Inc.
Published online in Wiley Online Library (wileyonlinelibrary.com) • DOI: 10.1002/tl.20123

deepen and enrich their ability to analyze and reflect on a subject, is broadly applicable to many disciplines. Second, the assignments outlined here, designed to sharpen students' observational and analytical skills with respect to moving images, might be adapted to any class that seeks to engage with visual material. Third, I hope that readers from all disciplines find resonance with the discussion of learning objectives that reach beyond the acquisition and application of foundational knowledge.

Objectives

I want to provide in my courses what L. Dee Fink calls a "significant learning experience," a process that fundamentally changes students (Fink 2003, 6). The integration of production activities helps students to develop visual literacy, which Deandra Little, Peter Felten, and Chad Berry (2010) argue is ever more important to a liberal education, and yet, often unaddressed in college-level courses. They write:

> At a young age, sighted individuals learn to "see" in ways that come to seem effortless and automatic. As teachers, we have a tendency to conflate this effortless seeing with visual literacy, assuming that students who possess the requisite baseline skills to "see" can, and therefore do, carefully observe and analyze each image before them. However, the often cursory attention students pay to the task of seeing a new image or re-seeing a familiar image is not sufficient to produce a detailed observation of what is there, let alone a sophisticated interpretation of what it might mean. (46)

Much of my own journey toward learning how to "see" happened not in college or graduate school, but while interning at video production companies. The hands-on experience of learning to shoot and edit had a profound impact on my understanding of the inner workings of film and video, and it still informs my scholarship today. As the tools of digital media production have become more accessible, I have worked to involve my students in their thoughtful use, hoping to provide a "natural critical learning environment" in which students' advanced language skills develop organically as their visual literacy and cultural knowledge deepen (Bain 2004, 18). Audiovisual expression and visual literacy more generally are becoming as important as writing and speaking for developing a professional presence in the world.

I have also come to value Fink's taxonomy of significant learning because it has helped me articulate some of my intangible dreams for my courses. To the classic categories of foundational and applied knowledge, Fink adds integration, the human dimension, caring, and learning how to learn as fundamental aspects of a deep learning experience (Fink 2003, 30). Making some of these goals explicit has helped me and my students track their progress on a wide range of competencies that are directly applicable to various personal and professional endeavors beyond the class. Articulating these goals has also led me to design assignments and activities that are aligned with my goals.

Foundational knowledge, in my discipline, means that students will become aware of, and engage deeply with, a particular body of cinematic work as well as learn to associate particular cinematic techniques with specific directors, movements, and moments in film history. I also expect them to leave my class being able to isolate and describe, using new vocabulary and concepts, the component elements that are specific to film and different from other forms of expression. They should be able to recognize when rules and conventions are being followed and when they are being broken.

My courses also work toward objectives that Fink might associate with the level of application. In a purely disciplinary context, I'd like students to ask and answer sophisticated questions about the relationship between a particular moment in a film and the overarching esthetic project of the whole work. Thinking more broadly across disciplines, they should become better prepared to tackle complex professional tasks; to speak and write the language of the course (whether their native language or another) with precision and accuracy; to improve their abilities to think creatively, critically, and practically; and to become better problem solvers, more competent project managers, and more effective team members on group projects.

Thinking more deeply about other levels of objectives that include integration of knowledge and the human dimension, I encourage students to articulate precisely what it is about a particular audiovisual work that evokes their personal response to it. I also work toward building their confidence in their own ability to produce high-quality creative work that is meaningful to themselves and compelling to others.

All of the above objectives appear in some form on my course syllabus. But I also have implicit hopes for my students' learning, hopes that involve a kind of personal engagement with the material that students will come to on their own, sometimes without realizing it, or only much later. These goals assemble loosely around Fink's ideas of caring and learning how to learn. I hope that students will come to appreciate the films studied in the class and will grow to seek out and value other films they may previously have found difficult or formally challenging. In an ideal world, they will also come to love the French language enough to seek out resources to help them master its complications. They will become deeply curious about the complex interplay among language, culture, and history, and willing to undertake their own explorations of the literary and geographical hinterlands of the French-speaking world. Moreover, they will come to honor their own creative impulses and seek out new avenues for personal self-expression. I even dream that they will feel happy when learning, even when the task is painstaking and the way ahead is not easily visible.

In the following discussion, I outline the assignments and activities I use to support my explicit and implicit objectives, with particular attention to the management of audiovisual assignments that may be less familiar to readers. I then describe in detail how the theory-practice model might look for one module of the course.

Course Design, Assignments, and Scaffolding

The image of today's college students as "digital natives" who make and understand films as easily as they breathe is only partially true. If asked to make a digital video project with no scaffolding, students will come back with something, as they would if asked to write an analytical article on cinema. However, students and instructors tend to underestimate the complexity of the medium and overestimate the "fun" assumed to accompany such assignments. The quality of their analytical and creative work can be improved through scaffolded assignments that are carefully aligned with the learning objectives.

Breaking down students' attention to a visual artifact into its component parts helps them to observe and describe detail more precisely, a key stage in being able to compile a more abstract and complex analysis. In the case of film and video, these parts include word, sound, image, editing, and so on. Following are a few examples of assignments that draw students' attention to individual elements of audiovisual expression.

To engage students in audiovisual expression and to begin building skills, I begin with simple, low-stakes audiovisual assignments. These assignments, using basic camera equipment, improve students' observational skills when analyzing cinema and improve their shooting skills when producing their own work. The assignments are narrowly focused on one concept or technique. Students must produce one or two very short video clips that illustrate the concept, often by contrasting several versions of the same subject. These assignments take little time, can be done in or outside of class, and focus the students' attention on detail. They also help steer students away from common shooting errors such as lack of tripod use, poor composition, improper lighting, ambient sound interference, or shooting vertical images with a cell phone. Students submit the clips electronically to the media management tool in our course management system, where they are then available for follow-up discussion in class. I often have students work on these assignments in class because linguistic acquisition is so central to my learning objectives, and it is easier to keep students working in the target language if they are flowing in and out of the classroom.

The specific content of this type of assignment varies according to course topic and objectives. For example, they might shoot a similar shot with and without a tripod, with and without proper lighting, with internal and external microphone, or with the subject positioned differently in the frame. Additional variations might include shooting one item from all different angles, capturing sound only from a certain location or event, constructing a simple story in five shots, or shooting a long-duration still shot. For this type of low-stakes assignment, I generally assign a completion grade.

A different, more analytical type of audiovisual assignment can provide opportunities for students to demonstrate their understanding of a broader concept covered in the course. For example, students might shoot exercises illustrating different documentary modes, borrowing techniques from one of the French New Wave directors, or demonstrating their understanding of a particular editing style. These analytical audiovisual assignments are a useful complement to the skill-building assignments and the analytical writing assignments in which students also engage regularly. Students submit these assignments with a written commentary explaining their objectives, and the grade evaluates the thinking behind the assignment rather than its technical execution.

Skill-building and analytical audiovisual assignments generally lead up to a more open-ended, creative final project. These projects are "high-stakes" graded assignments in which both conceptual sophistication and production quality matter. In order to guide students toward high-quality digital work, it is important to provide guidelines on story development, as well as shooting, editing, and the use of copyrighted material.

Whether students are working in fiction, documentary, or any combination of the two, they need time to develop their story/argument, which is fundamental to the quality of the final product. This aspect is important to any digital video assignment in any discipline. Over the course of several weeks early in the semester, I include fifteen-minute in-class sessions on story/argument development. Initially, they bring to class three ideas for projects, which they discuss in small groups along with questions borrowed from Joe Lambert et al.'s (2010) excellent manual, *The Digital Storytelling Cookbook*. Later, they select one of those ideas and discuss it in small groups, again responding to a series of questions about what the story means and why it matters. I repeat this process several times with different groups early in the semester, before students start work on the writing and production of their films, in order to guide students toward a viable project idea. Students then submit successive versions of their project in writing, to which I provide written feedback, and as the script progresses, they submit as many drafts as necessary in order to polish the language.

To prepare them for the shooting phase of the project, we develop the skills needed to capture well-crafted images in the skill-building assignments discussed earlier. However, when shooting for a final project, students often encounter unexpected difficulties such as unsuitable weather and scheduling conflicts. Planning for these eventualities warrants an explicit deadline for the completion of shooting built into the schedule. This allows the instructor to monitor students' progress and help them solve problems.

If the project is simple, students require little training with editing software. However, it is useful to build in some time for in-class editing, as this is a good chance for students to work with each other and to discuss their projects informally with the instructor. This informal laboratory-like experience builds a strong group dynamic in the class. Editing is analogous to revision in writing, and by working together in the same room, students come to feel they are part of a team striving for the best possible result for every project. In second-language classes, editing sessions are prime opportunities for sustained project-based learning in the target language. Students use and reuse both the film vocabulary and the computer vocabulary they have learned in the course.

Editing is also the stage where students often want to add images or music to refine their final project. This is the time to bring up copyright issues. I encourage them to exclude all copyrighted material and to have broader aspirations for their work beyond the class. I encourage them to make their own images or music, or to ask friends for permission to use their creative work. Students learn to seek out websites where artists explicitly grant permission to reuse their work, and they check for Creative Commons licensing and cite their sources for any material that is not original.

I assign grades to final projects using course-specific rubrics. Examples of the categories I might include in a rubric are creativity/risk, story/structure, writing quality, image quality, sound quality, and editing/rhythm. I always try to publish the projects in an online gallery and encourage students to post them to a public online media site as well.

Despite the audiovisual assignments I have added to my film courses, I have not reduced the amount of writing. Not all of the writing assignments take the form of exams or essays, however. Students write and revise their project proposals and scripts multiple times, they comment on their audiovisual exercises in writing, they select film clips from the required viewing list and comment on them, they write an in-class scene analysis essay on an unfamiliar clip, and they write a final essay about their completed film. Through these writing assignments, they practice the same writing skills needed for the five-page essays I used to assign: planning, writing, and revision; argumentation, observation, and description; clarity and accuracy in French. However, in the new format, the skills are mixed and matched in different ways, and the overall quality of the writing has improved.

Sample Course Module Design: Framing and Composition

In the blended theory-practice model, my courses are broken down into modules isolating different elements of audiovisual expression such as framing and composition, sound, and editing. Each module opens and closes with analytical work (reading/viewing/writing/discussion), with practical exercises woven in along the way. Following is an example of how one such module, devoted to framing and composition, might flow over the course of two to three weeks.

NEW DIRECTIONS FOR TEACHING AND LEARNING • DOI: 10.1002/tl

The framing and composition module opens with a theoretical reading on the subject and the screening of a visually compelling film. Claire Denis's *Beau travail* (1999) or Jacques Perrin's *Le peuple migrateur/Winged Migration* (2001), fiction and documentary, respectively, are examples from the French corpus. In other disciplines, I would select a film in which the visual element (as opposed to plot, theme, sound, and so on) seems to be particularly salient. Class opens with a short clip (no more than one minute) that I ask students to describe. I stay on this clip far longer than they might expect, prompting students to look for elements they might not have mentioned at first (such as lines, negative space, movement of the frame or within the frame, colors, and lighting). I try to keep them in purely descriptive mode for a while, before moving into analytical mode with questions about why these choices were made, how they create meaning, and how we as viewers respond to them. I often link the discussion back to concepts in the reading at this point, with a few minutes of lecture on the frame, off-screen and on-screen space, depth of field, and other visual concepts.

A small group discussion follows. In groups of two to four, students watch another clip, inventory all the visual elements, and discuss the reasons behind these choices. I circulate as they talk, then compare results in a quick full-group discussion. The small group work allows everyone in the room to participate actively in the identification and description of key compositional elements and the practice of situating these elements within a broader analytical frame. It also gives every student a chance to practice his/her oral French (or, in the case of a course in students' native language, to practice their oral language skills in this new domain of knowledge).

The next part of the unit is a short illustrated lecture on the practical elements of composition. Students read a "how-to" text on composition (such as Schroeppel's [2003] *The Bare Bones Camera Course for Film and Video*), and I explain how and why one might want to make a "good-quality" composition. I introduce topics such as background and depth of field, attention to lines, rule of thirds, use of space, color and lighting, importance of stability, attention to space for gaze/movement, and avoiding the vertically framed "cell phone" shot. Students then shoot a visual assignment demonstrating their attention to the lessons learned. Drawing from topics covered under the "skill-building assignments" section above, I ask students to submit a visual demonstration of two or three contrasting compositions of the same subject. Students upload their clips to the class media gallery and we view and discuss them as a group.

Next, we either return to discussion of the earlier film or another film. I generally find that the sophistication of visual observation and analysis has increased exponentially. Students then do a writing assignment such as a close analysis of a self-selected or instructor-selected clip, and I find a concurrent increase in the level of precision and detail in the written analyses.

NEW DIRECTIONS FOR TEACHING AND LEARNING • DOI: 10.1002/tl

Tools and Technical Notes

Many of these assignments can be done with simple camera equipment. If using phones or other tiny cameras, it is important to have light tripods available. If one of the objectives is to encourage students to appreciate quality and to pursue it in their audiovisual work, it can be useful to have some higher-quality options available. I found that even beginners aspired to produce better images and sound once they had used excellent cameras and external microphones. For editing, I tend to keep things simple, encouraging students to use a program they are familiar with.

Assessment/Results

I am encouraged to continue with this kind of teaching because of several indicators. The first is that despite the increased workload I now expect of my students, I receive no complaints about the quantity of work. Second, students' work, both in written and audiovisual form, is of higher quality than it was in earlier courses. I think students are performing better because they are more engaged and more motivated to perfect their work. Recently, one student approached me after the final screenings and asked if she could go back and add to her final essay, which had already been graded. She had some new thoughts she wanted to share with me, and she was not concerned with any grading incentive.

Additional encouragement appears in students' comments on evaluations. Many perceive that their analytical approach to film and video has improved dramatically, often reporting they will never watch a film the same way again. One student wrote, "The most amazing thing about this class is the knowledge that I gained [...] I have always watched videos etc. and never appreciated the components and what it added to the meaning/implicit sense of the video. We always try to interpret written words, but digital media is just as rich with symbols and meaning." Some students also report progress on some of my implicit objectives. One wrote that the class was "also applicable to other classes/life," another stated that "this class really helped me want to do more filmmaking," and several recently expressed a desire to seek out more French films to watch on their own. This semester, one student commented on taking away "the *worth* of doing creative things through art and writing," and another wrote, "I did things that made me happy that I haven't had time to do since being in college." These kinds of comments, sometimes followed up with cards, gifts, and thank-you notes from students, are more frequent then they were in more traditional versions of the course. Furthermore, students' perceptions of me as an approachable, caring instructor have increased. With improvements in performance and in their perceptions of performance, students appear to be learning something both they and I value.

Undertaking a complete course redesign, particularly one that involves digital technology, is an ambitious undertaking. I advocate an incremental

approach, making one or two changes per semester using tools with which the instructor is personally comfortable. Over time, as these small changes accumulate, we may begin to notice our students looking, and perhaps even thinking, differently.

References

Bain, K. 2004. *What the Best College Teachers Do*. Cambridge, MA: Harvard University Press.
Denis, C. 1999. *Beau travail* [Video]. Paris, France: Pyramide Distribution. (Available from New Yorker Films, New York, NY, 2000.)
Fink, L. D. 2003. *Creating Significant Learning Experiences: An Integrated Approach to Designing College Courses*. Hoboken, NJ: Wiley.
Lambert, J., A. Hill, N. Mullen, C. Paull, E. Paulos, T. Soundararajan, and D. Weinshenker. 2010. *The Digital Storytelling Cookbook*. Berkeley, CA: The Digital Diner Press.
Little, D., P. Felten, and C. Berry. 2010. "Liberal Education in a Visual World." *Liberal Education* 96 (2): 44–49.
Perrin, J. 2001. *Le peuple migrateur/Winged Migration* [Video]. Paris, France: Bac Films. (Available from Maple Pictures, Toronto, 2010.)
Schroeppel, T. 2003. *The Bare Bones Camera Course for Film and Video*. Tampa, FL: Author.

ALISON J. MURRAY LEVINE is the Horace W. Goldsmith Distinguished Teaching Professor of French at the University of Virginia.

Understanding how to critique visual images can be beneficial for faculty teaching in art, design, or visual communication fields, but also for any faculty who use images to teach course content.

Learning—to and from—the Visual Critique Process

Phillip Motley

Introduction

Critiquing visual images is vital to the development of future art, design, and visual communication practitioners, as well as to the general development of any student's visual literacy skills. In my visual communication courses, a critique is a defined process in which the creator has a visual artifact assessed by others through a method characterized by observation, reflection, and verbal articulation. In other environments, particularly those where learning is not predicated on image creation, critiques can be used to examine image-based cultural or historical artifacts as a means to better learn course content. The same might apply when students are required to create or manipulate visual images, but for purposes that aren't specifically focused on the images themselves. For example, a student tasked with creating a visual presentation about a historical event or scientific process might need to evaluate and select images for use in a slide deck. Through the critique process, students—and teachers—are able to tease out the inherent strengths and weaknesses of possible images to better ground topical discussions in virtually any discipline or to help develop more effective presentations.

A critique can take various forms. I implement critiques in my classes in a variety of ways including pin-up critiques—groups of images pinned to a wall and evaluated together; formal critique presentations—individually presented and reviewed final project artifacts; and peer-review workshop critiques—small-group reviews of in-progress projects performed without my direct involvement. Regardless of structure, assessment lies at the heart of all critiques whether they are used to evaluate generated images or pre-existing artifacts. In contrast to the summative assessment of art criticism, critiques are usually formative in nature, designed to help students improve their abilities to create images (Eisner 2002) or to think critically about an

NEW DIRECTIONS FOR TEACHING AND LEARNING, no. 141, Spring 2015 © 2015 Wiley Periodicals, Inc.
Published online in Wiley Online Library (wileyonlinelibrary.com) • DOI: 10.1002/tl.20124

image's inherent qualities. The process can vary in focus—general issues or specific criteria—or in who does the assessing—from faculty-led critiques to ones where faculty and students contribute equally. Critiques can explore an image as a singular artifact or within a broader context.

Critiques are by design practice-based; the more frequently students participate in critiques the better they get at the process. Critiques are most useful to the development of an image when they are performed iteratively throughout a task. They can be held when the image being created is complete, but also at the beginning or midstream of its development or usage. In my classes, I seldom call for a critique only at the end of a project as students benefit greatly from the opportunity to evaluate their decisions throughout the creative process. In order to enhance learning, especially when the primary objective is concerned with encouraging critical thinking skills—rather than with the image itself—students should be asked to critique often to develop necessary observation, reflection, and articulation abilities. However, the repetitive nature of regular critiques can dull even the most attentive students' abilities in this regard. A continual challenge for instructors, then, is to design ways to make critiques lively, engaging, and productive.

Origins of Critique

Critique has a long history and can be used for different purposes, from exploratory description of a visual image to interpretive or analytical assessment of a work. Some of the earliest mentions of art criticism come from architectural competitions during the Renaissance (Elkins 2001). Critiques of visual images are derived from the broader field of art criticism and are a product of Romantic period master classes that were held in direct response to the authoritarian designations of quality from the preceding Baroque period (Elkins 2001).

Smith (1973) describes two basic forms of criticism: exploratory—activities based on description, analysis, characterization, and interpretation—and argumentative—activities based on evaluation, argument, and defense. Both forms have pedagogical implications for critiques: exploratory critiques are concerned with what an image is about, while argumentative critiques focus on evaluating whether an image is good or not (Barrett 2000). Freedman (2003) summarizes the process: critique is "a form of social knowledge production done in the context of a cultural milieu of art program evaluation and student assessment" (7).

The process of critiquing visual images created by students has a long relationship with arts instruction. It is a process fully devoted to assessment (either summative or formative) that is sometimes concerned with specific aesthetic or technical criteria and at other times with the content itself. Critiques are believed to be crucial to the creation of high-quality visual images and hold a place of prominence within art programs. Both exploratory and argumentative critiques can be found in most fine arts courses and are integrated into the curriculum from beginning to advanced levels (Barrett 2000; Klebesadel and Kornetsky 2009). In addition to the fine arts, many design fields—graphic design, architecture, product design, and so on—follow a similar critique-driven pedagogy (Barrett 2000). Critiques are also an important aspect of professions where visual images are created, including graphic design, advertising, and web design. Learning how to critique through practice in the classroom, then, can help prepare students for future careers.

Broad approaches to critique often make sense for many reasons, in particular due to the importance visual imagery occupies in current culture. The study of visual imagery is no longer the strict province of the arts. Programs in a wide range of design, communications, and visual studies fields produce, employ, and analyze visual images. This may suggest a relaxing of some of the constraints traditionally found in fine art critiques and further indicate that critiquing a wide breadth of imagery can be beneficial for students (Freedman 2003). It also suggests the potential value of the critique process to students learning about topics that exist well beyond the boundaries that surround art and design disciplines.

Pedagogy

For educational purposes, critiques can help students see their own work clearly, understand its strengths and weaknesses, and determine problems they have not perceived on their own. Students learning to design, manipulate, or use visual images need to develop critical thinking and language skills necessary for describing both the merits and weaknesses of a given visual artifact (Klebesadel and Kornetsky 2009). This is true whether the artifact is created by an individual student, one of his or her classmates, or by a professional. In general, critiques possess specific qualities: they are focused—activities center around specific works; reflective—students must consider what is successful and why; verbal—students must articulate their observations; and forward-looking—critiques are designed for improving future efforts (Hetland et al. 2007). In my own courses, I organize critiques for two main reasons: to help students improve their images by exposing them to views and options that might not be part of their normal thoughts and routines or to qualitatively assess a visual artifact in its completed form.

The critique is a primarily social act; though an individual can perform a self-critique, the process normally involves at least two people, often many more. Frequently organized around a group, critiques can also be done individually, one on one between an instructor and a student, or between pairs or small groups of students (Barrett 2000). Regardless of the number of participants, critiques involve reciprocal relationships between the student and faculty member and also between students themselves (Eisner 2002). In a critique, students can be required to frame their images prior to commentary or to simply present their work for analysis without any supporting description. Likewise, in a course where production of images is not a central goal, images can be presented by the instructor (or student) for examination and discussion by the class. Consistent throughout all these variations, critiques are organized to stimulate critical discussions and assessment of a visual image's qualities.

Critiques are also inherently comparative. Hetland et al. (2007) state, "Generally, observing in critiques involves looking at your own work in the context of pieces created by other students or in relation to multiple drawings of your own" (104). The acts of observation, reflection, comparison, and verbal articulation can be viewed, then, as specialized forms of critical thinking where visual images are central to the process. In my classes, I want students to make aesthetic and critical judgments that synthesize what they observe visually with what they have been taught. Critiques can be a good solution for this goal as visual images can be discussed in a variety of ways—what the content represents; what communication methods are implemented; or how specific principles are employed. The use of progressive critiques—ones that occur midstream of a project—can facilitate just-in-time discussions of issues significant to a particular stage of an image's development. Critiques can be structured to allow for concentrated discussions of only a few standards that address specific assignment criteria or stages of the creative process.

The public display of visuals (presentations, exhibitions, talks, and so on) can be a useful analog to a critique for all students, not just those learning how to create images. The public display of a visual image may not be exactly the same as having it critiqued, yet the process still requires reflection and consideration. Students viewing images they have produced or selected through the eyes of others are often compelled to reconsider their work as a whole, see it from a fresh perspective, and discover issues they didn't previously perceive.

Three Types of Critique

There are three main types of critiques that should be discussed further: critiques of professionally created images, critiques of images created by student peers, and critiques of self-produced images.

Critiquing Professional Work. For a typical student, learning to critique the work of professionals can often be the easiest. Examining professional work, whether contemporary or historical, helps students recognize the hallmarks of an effective image. When evaluating the work of students, instructors often make comparisons to professional work as a way of articulating a particular point (Hetland et al. 2007). Critiquing professional work allows students to practice perceiving particular qualities of an artifact and then helps them verbalize their observations using discipline-specific vocabulary. For example, in a graduate course on visual aesthetics, I introduce the critique process by asking students to select professionally created images pertaining to a selected topic or technique. As we critique the professional work, I encourage the students to use terminology that is germane to the topics we are currently studying in class. Sometimes I give students rubrics or other tools to help them identify specific issues in professional images that align with a current assignment. After using the tool, I ask students to summarize the images they critiqued and map significant observations to their own image development process. This helps them connect the current state of their own efforts to the quality of work they aspire to create and provides the opportunity to mimic the practices they judge successful.

Critiquing professional work can be useful at encouraging students to refrain from typical forms of praise (for example, "I like it") to more sophisticated language that describes specific positive and negative aspects of an image (Barrett 2000; Freedman 2003). According to Eisner (2002), "The greater the need to comment, the greater the need to search the work in order to have something to say. Sight breeds language, and language breeds sight" (194). Critiquing professional work helps students understand this form of comparison and can guide them toward more sophisticated choices with their own work.

In my experience, students are more comfortable analyzing and discussing professional images simply because the creator is not present during the critique. They are free to comment as they wish without the anxieties that emerge when they judge their own work or the work of their peers. Asking students to critique work from fields different from what they are studying often motivates them to seek solutions to visual problems from uncommon sources (Barrett 1988; Freedman 2003). For example, I have found that exposing graphic design students to works of fine art often leads them to make divergent choices with the images they create.

Critiquing Peers.   Critiquing images created by classmates can be more challenging for some students. During critiques, students are asked to consider classmates' images and then provide feedback to their peers. In many cases, the work submitted by a classmate is not of uniform high quality and thus benefits from both positive and negative comments. This type of critique requires a student to integrate assigned criteria with observations of the visual properties present, and then articulate an assessment. This can be difficult, especially for beginners. Novices often respond through instinct rather than reasoned consideration, which can lead to awkward or even damaging comments. Nonetheless, critiquing peers can be beneficial to students when they are able to synthesize the observations they make about peers' work with their own efforts (Klebesadel and Kornetsky 2009).

For some students, feelings of social pressure add to the difficulty of offering honest and authentic feedback, especially when that feedback is negative. Classrooms can be highly social environments, ones where students are reluctant to say anything constructive or negative about a peer for reasons of social standing (Freedman 2003; Hetland et al. 2007). However, the need to surmount this challenge is important. Disingenuous feedback is rarely useful to a student; instead, it can be misleading or even damaging if the assessment isn't accurate or true. My own experiences with critiques in classes that range from the freshman–sophomore level to the graduate level suggest that the social dynamic of a critique is generally tied to the maturity of the students involved. Coaching graduate students to abandon platitudes in favor of more cerebral—and thus valuable—comments is less challenging than it is with younger students. When the critique process happens often and regularly, students become better at dispensing with language that is primarily laudatory and instead provide feedback that is genuine and constructive.

Often the best critiques occur when students are willing to challenge their peers' assertions. When students feel compelled to defend their decisions against peer observations, they must use rhetoric and persuasion to convey their views. This, again, requires critical thinking, articulation, and mastery of disciplinary vocabulary (Hetland et al. 2007). To help keep critiques as emotionally neutral as possible, I regularly remind students to offer feedback that is objective—not personal.

Self-Critiques.   For some students, the process of critiquing their own work is the most difficult of the three methods; it is also, perhaps, the most important. Instructors, informed peers, or colleagues who can assist with evaluation aren't always available, yet the need for objective assessment is a constant pressure for students as they create visual imagery. Therefore, students must cultivate an ability to dispassionately and objectively critique their own efforts. Over many years of implementing critiques, I have found this to be one of the most difficult aspects of the process to teach. Students who excel at critiquing others can have great difficulty doing the same with their own work. For many students, disengaging from the effort and ego poured into creating a visual image in order to clearly see the merits of the piece is a difficult but necessary step. I have found that first learning to critique peer and professional work helps students develop the critical analysis abilities they need when they later attempt to pinpoint problematic aspects of their own work. Likewise, learning how to be critiqued can help students develop the "thick skin" needed to eventually critique themselves effectively.

Challenges and Best Practices

Recognizing the challenges endemic to many critiques can help faculty from all disciplines design productive learning opportunities for students. One-on-one critiques are hard for many students because of the intense involvement required. Because the responsibility for communication cannot be avoided, students in a one-on-one critique quickly realize the limits of their vocabulary or understanding of disciplinary issues. When I perform

NEW DIRECTIONS FOR TEACHING AND LEARNING • DOI: 10.1002/tl

one-on-one critiques, less assertive or articulate students struggle since choosing to let peers do most of the talking isn't an option.

Group critiques suffer for opposing reasons: the many voices involved can potentially minimize any individual's observations. Group critiques can drag on; they begin full of energy but often become stilted and repetitive as time passes. Students start by giving great feedback to peers with those critiqued early in a session receiving thoughtful and useful comments. Students critiqued later, however, often receive less valuable comments. Repetition sometimes leads to overly obvious, even cliché comments.

Self-critiques are also challenging. Sometimes it is hard for students to see the true nature of their work. Students who work hard at developing a visual image can easily become convinced of their own logic and reasoning—even when flawed. Discovering ways to be objective and force oneself to be honest can be difficult. Yet the repercussions of not doing so, especially when students' only reliable evaluators are themselves, can be costly. In my experience, helping students develop the skills to self-critique effectively is the most difficult aspect of the process to teach. I often require students to write about their visual work—through journals, blogs, or other reflection-focused activities—in response to provided prompts as a means to help make their evaluative process explicit.

To facilitate the most learning from the process for students, I suggest that faculty give extra consideration to three aspects of a critique: practical, cognitive, and interpersonal issues.

Practical Issues.   There are practical issues to consider when conducting a critique. Sticking to a predefined time limit is a simple, but effective, way to ensure that critiques are productive and full of fresh and lively commentary. It is time consuming—and tiring—to critique a classroom full of students during a single meeting. Rather than fill an entire class session with a critique, faculty can instead extend the critique over more than one period. Multiple short but intense critiques are sometimes more effective than one long session.

Unless the critique is a final, summative assessment, students also benefit when they are given time to work further on their images in the same period in which their work is critiqued. This approach is useful for the students being critiqued but can also be productive for the ones giving the critique. Students who make thoughtful observations about a peer's image are often able to see their own efforts in new ways afterward.

Finding ways to introduce variety into the critique process can encourage students to develop a greater appetite—and tolerance—for a repetitive and time-consuming process. The following list describes several variations on the standard critique that I have used in my own classes:

- Speed-date critiques where students, working in tandem for three to five minutes, assess each other's images. As this approach allows students to share their work with a large number of peers in a short amount of time,

I find it to be most useful in the middle of a project when students might be stuck and will benefit from suggestions.

- Peer-workshop critiques where groups of three to four students take turns interrogating each other's work. I use this approach to help students develop a sense of collaborative reflection and articulation as they must share and negotiate their differing observations and opinions about each group member's work.

- Pin-up critiques where students collectively display their images tacked to a wall. In this type of critique, the discussion is allowed to move freely from image to image. I use this variation in beginner-level courses because it allows students to easily develop solutions by comparing and contrasting their work with classmates' projects.

- Self-assessment critiques in which students use a tool to evaluate how their work aligns with assigned requirements. I employ this approach to help students—usually at a more advanced level—develop the objectivity needed to successfully critique their own work.

- Group critiques with invited professionals. This can be instructive as experts often bring concerns from the professional world to bear on discussions during the critique. I find that invited guests often reinforce important ideas that I have shared with students previously.

Cognitive Issues.   Whether students are on the giving or receiving end, critiques should incorporate learning objectives that promote critical thinking skills. Critiques require students to analyze and think critically about the inherent qualities of an image. Critiques that turn into prescriptive problem-solving sessions are rarely effective. Solving problems with an image is the responsibility of the creator, not the student making the observations. A critique becomes valuable to the greater learning goals of a class when students receiving a critique are able to synthesize received feedback along with their own ideas within the larger contextual framework of the course. Providing time for students to address their work in the same class session in which the critique occurred can allow students to maximize feedback they receive.

To promote learning about visual images, it helps to have students first describe what they are attempting to create. In my classes, this often means having students state the particular goals of their projects followed by their assessments of what is and isn't working. If students aren't sure or are unable to articulate this information, then the critique—and the project—is often ineffective. Finding mechanisms that insert space between students' goals for an image and the reality of its current state often allows them to see the image from a fresh perspective. Without this type of opportunity, students run the risk of becoming lost in the minutiae of their own ideas.

Critiquing skills can be valuable to students beyond a particular course or project. The process develops observational abilities, promotes reflection, and demands intelligent verbalization. Faculty can prepare students for this type of activity prior to a scheduled critique. I often ask students to assess their own work in writing prior to a critique by describing their broad goals for the image, their evaluations of the piece's current strengths and weaknesses, and the issues slowing their progress. A simpler approach can be to ask students to come up with a handful of questions about their images that they want addressed during a critique (Barrett 2000). Intentional activities like these can help transform a critique into a more productive process for students.

Interpersonal Issues.   As the critique process is usually a social one, interpersonal issues are also important to consider. A paucity of diverse views can hamper a well-intentioned critique. A critique characterized by rich ideas, bold but fair statements, and a multitude of views can turn a sedate critique into a valuable, even inspiring, event. It's important for participants to abide by a shared set of social practices that support—not hinder—the attributes of a good critique: honest, clear discussions driven by keen observations and considered reflections, which result in constructive feedback.

I find it beneficial to provide a set of guidelines for both giving and receiving critiques to students prior to a first critique in a course. Guidelines can also be developed together with students. Differences between constructive criticism and personal attacks should be discussed as that distinction sometimes becomes blurred, especially for students new to the process. It is important to help students understand that how they communicate their observations can be just as important as the views themselves. Unless the critique requires an oral defense, students receiving the feedback should agree not to take things personally and to quell the desire to argue points being made by a faculty member or peer.

Students often wrestle with issues of social standing during critiques. This is usually manifested in how students attempt to communicate sensitive information to each other. I implement anonymous forms for written feedback, which allows students to provide their classmates with comments they might not want to communicate verbally during class. Another possibility is to use "round-robin" style critiques where students leave their work and blank paper at their desk and then receive anonymous written feedback as they and their peers circulate the room.

Conclusion

Though critiques are primarily found in art or design focused courses or in professional environments, the skills they instill in students can be useful beyond the act of interrogating a visual image. Sharpening students' powers of observation, increasing the depths of their reflections, and cultivating their abilities to offer meaningful and actionable feedback to other students are valuable in most courses. Faculty who require students to create some form of artifact—not just those related to the arts but also reports, narratives, or presentations—might benefit from studying the process and structure of the critique.

References

Barrett, T. 1988. "A Comparison of the Goals of Studio Professors Conducting Critiques and Art Education Goals for Teaching Criticism." *Studies in Art Education* 30 (1): 22–27.

Barrett, T. 2000. "Studio Critiques of Student Art: As They Are, as They Could Be with Mentoring." *Theory Into Practice* 39 (1): 29–35.

Eisner, E. W. 2002. *The Arts and the Creation of Mind.* New Haven, CT: Yale University Press.

Elkins, J. 2001. *Why Art Cannot Be Taught: A Handbook for Art Students.* Chicago, IL: University of Illinois Press.

Freedman, K. 2003. *Teaching Visual Culture: Curriculum, Aesthetics and the Social Life of Art.* New York, NY: Teachers College Press.

Hetland, L., E. Winner, S. Veenema, and K. M. Sheridan. 2007. *Studio Thinking: The Real Benefits of Visual Arts Education.* New York, NY: Teachers College Press.

Klebesadel, H., and L. Kornetsky. 2009. "Critique as Signature Pedagogy in the Arts." In *Exploring Signature Pedagogies: Approaches to Teaching Disciplinary Habits of Mind,* edited by R. Gurung, N. Chick, and A. Haynie, 99–120. Sterling, VA: Stylus.

Smith, R. A. 1973. "Teaching Aesthetic Criticism in the Schools." *Journal of Aesthetic Education* 7 (1): 38–49.

PHILLIP MOTLEY is an associate professor of communications at Elon University.

8

This final chapter highlights seven general suggestions and strategies for faculty (and others) working to develop visual literacy in classrooms and across the curriculum. The chapters throughout this volume illustrate and elaborate on these strategies; they are condensed here as a quick guide to effective practice.

Teaching Visual Literacy across the Curriculum: Suggestions and Strategies

Deandra Little

Throughout this volume, the authors of each chapter point out a number of specific ways they teach students to learn by looking in a variety of contexts. This final chapter highlights seven general suggestions and strategies for faculty (and others) working to develop visual literacy in classrooms and across the curriculum.[1] The chapters throughout this volume illustrate and elaborate on these seven strategies; they are condensed here as a quick guide to effective practice.

Consider Carefully How Visual Analysis or Creation Helps Students Meet Your Learning Goals and Objectives

As the chapter authors demonstrate, determining which learning goals or outcomes you want to teach with or through visual images is the first step in deciding how and when to use them in your courses. The following questions may help as you decide what students need to "see" and why:

- *Learning within a discipline.* How are images used in your discipline? What kind of images does your discipline use to make meaning? Do your students bring to class any relevant experience with those disciplinary images, or will you need to teach them the basics of reading that visual form?
- *Learning general skills associated with liberal education.* What general learning goals do you want to use images to teach or reinforce? Do you, for example, want students to develop their critical thinking skills by asking questions of a photo and beginning to understand how political images "work" in the popular media? Do you want students to write in response to a still or moving image to practice their observational and

New Directions for Teaching and Learning, no. 141, Spring 2015 © 2015 Wiley Periodicals, Inc.
Published online in Wiley Online Library (wileyonlinelibrary.com) • DOI: 10.1002/tl.20125

analytical skills? Or, do you want them to improve their self-expression by making images, drafting digital stories, or writing creatively in response to an image? What relevant visual literacy experiences or skills do students bring to your class from their experiences in other courses or in their lives outside of college?

Plan Assignments or Classroom Activities That Align with Your Goals or Outcomes

Ensure that students are building toward your learning goals by carefully considering how and why you are including images and visual literacy exercises in your classes, and how you are asking students to use or interact with them.

- How will, for example, analyzing, selecting, and/or creating visuals develop students' visual communication or critical thinking skills?
- How are you using images in your classroom—are they merely illustrations to provide variety, are they artifacts that students must interpret and manipulate to understand a particular concept or body of information, or are they fundamental to making meaning of the material, unit, or course?
- How will students practice the skills they need to master for assignments requiring visual analysis or production?

Consider the Ways in Which Experts and Novices "See" Differently

Remember that what we see isn't necessarily what students will see. Our disciplinary expertise means that we see patterns and derive meaning from particular visuals quickly and seemingly effortlessly, while students still have to learn how to analyze or produce visual images in disciplined and disciplinary ways. Although some visual literacy skills develop automatically over a lifetime of contact with images, the ones students develop out of habit tend to emphasize lower-order thinking skills. Research suggests that true proficiency or higher-order visual literacy does not develop unless these skills are identified and taught (Ausburn and Ausburn 1978). Consider:

- Who are your students, and what knowledge, skills, and beliefs are they bringing to your class that might affect what and how they see and interpret visual material? What habits have they developed, either in school or on social media, about interpreting or creating images?
- What visual skills do students need to practice in order to move from novice toward expert in your class?
- What might stand in the way of their learning? That is, what habits or ways of looking might they need to "unlearn" in order to do so?
- What specific observational or visual communication skills will help them learn to look with increasing complexity and sophistication?

Scaffold Assignments to Help Students Develop Visual and Disciplinary Expertise

After you have determined what kinds of assignments and activities will help students build the types of expertise that match your goals or outcomes, consider the order, complexity, and timing of these assignments. One clear progression might be asking students to practice visual communication skills early in the term with more straightforward images or assignments before moving on to more complex ones. You can then troubleshoot by assessing what they learn along the way and make adjustments as necessary. Beyond an individual classroom, if you are teaching with images across a program or curriculum, consider how students' interactions with images build from an introductory course to more advanced ones, or how work with images in different disciplines can be complementary. Exposure to varied, increasingly complex images coupled with thought-provoking discussions of them helps students learn how to make meaning of and meaning with visuals.

Model Professional Integrity for Image Use, and Help Students Understand Current Ethical and Legal Practices

Whether you already frequently display and share images in your courses or you have plans to do more, modeling good practices while displaying or analyzing visuals is key; your classroom or online activities should reflect current copyright rules and should show students how to appropriately cite visual sources. Librarians and instructional technologists at your campus can help you navigate Fair Use and multimedia composition. They can also work with you to access visual resources and image databases.

Make Visual Literacy a Long-Term Part of Your Teaching Practice, and Work Steadily over Time to Develop the Skills and Resources You Need to Help You Teach and Your Students Learn

Whether you are already teaching with images and want to refine an assignment here or there, or you have ambitious plans to rethink an entire course or program, carefully consider when, where, and how fully you want to integrate visual literacy into your work.

- What pace makes the most sense for you? Can you implement in phases by testing and refining an assignment or two, rather than planning a full-scale revision?
- What technological tools will students need to know how to use to succeed at any assignment? How and when will they learn to use those?
- What campus or online resources are available to help you teach and your students learn using visual sources and tools?

Make connections. Faculty colleagues, librarians, teaching and learning center staff, technologists, and others can help you locate images, articulate disciplinary outcomes, develop visual literacy exercises, and access the tools and databases you and your students will use.

Consider Ways to Share What You and Your Students Learn with Others

As you evaluate how well the changes you made helped students learn, plan early how you might share your emerging expertise with a campus colleague, at a conference, or through a scholarship of teaching and learning publication. Applying for Institutional Review Board approval before the semester starts and planning how you will capture, measure, and describe student learning can contribute not only to your students' learning but also to our understanding of teaching and learning more broadly.

- How does the course, assignment, or demonstrated student learning contribute back to your discipline or to your own practice?
- What did you learn about your students' learning that might help advance broader understanding of visual literacy or teaching and learning in your discipline?

Because visual literacy is still emerging as a concern in many disciplines and on many campuses, we have much to learn about how students learn and what teaching practices are most effective. The work you do in your classes and with your colleagues can contribute to the growing body of knowledge on the development of visual literacy within the disciplines and across the curriculum.

Note

1. Portions of this chapter are adapted from "Seeing Is Believing: Visual Teaching and Learning" (Little and Felten 2010).

References

Ausburn, L. J., and F. B. Ausburn. 1978. "Visual Literacy: Background Theory and Practice." *Programmed Learning and Educational Technology* 15: 291–297.

Little, D., and P. Felten. 2010. "Seeing Is Believing: Visual Teaching and Learning." *NEA Higher Education Advocate (Thriving in Academe)* 28: 5–8.

DEANDRA LITTLE directs the Center for the Advancement of Teaching and Learning and is an associate professor of English at Elon University.

INDEX

NEW DIRECTIONS FOR TEACHING AND LEARNING
ORDER FORM SUBSCRIPTION AND SINGLE ISSUES

DISCOUNTED BACK ISSUES:

Use this form to receive 20% off all back issues of *New Directions for Teaching and Learning*.
All single issues priced at **$23.20** (normally $29.00)

TITLE	ISSUE NO.	ISBN
_____	_____	_____
_____	_____	_____
_____	_____	_____

Call 1-800-835-6770 or see mailing instructions below. When calling, mention the promotional code JBNND
to receive your discount. For a complete list of issues, please visit www.josseybass.com/go/ndtl

SUBSCRIPTIONS: (1 YEAR, 4 ISSUES)

☐ New Order   ☐ Renewal

U.S.	☐ Individual: $89	☐ Institutional: $335
CANADA/MEXICO	☐ Individual: $89	☐ Institutional: $375
ALL OTHERS	☐ Individual: $113	☐ Institutional: $409

Call 1-800-835-6770 or see mailing and pricing instructions below.
Online subscriptions are available at www.onlinelibrary.wiley.com

ORDER TOTALS:

Issue / Subscription Amount: $ _____

Shipping Amount: $ _____
(for single issues only – subscription prices include shipping)

Total Amount: $ _____

SHIPPING CHARGES:

First Item $6.00
Each Add'l Item $2.00

(No sales tax for U.S. subscriptions. Canadian residents, add GST for subscription orders. Individual rate subscriptions must
be paid by personal check or credit card. Individual rate subscriptions may not be resold as library copies.)

BILLING & SHIPPING INFORMATION:

☐ **PAYMENT ENCLOSED:** *(U.S. check or money order only. All payments must be in U.S. dollars.)*

☐ **CREDIT CARD:**   ☐ VISA   ☐ MC   ☐ AMEX

Card number _____ Exp. Date _____

Card Holder Name_____ Card Issue # _____

Signature _____ Day Phone _____

☐ **BILL ME:** *(U.S. institutional orders only. Purchase order required.)*

Purchase order # _____
Federal Tax ID 13559302 • GST 89102-8052

Name _____

Address_____

Phone_____ E-mail_____

Copy or detach page and send to: **John Wiley & Sons, One Montgomery Street, Suite 1000,**
San Francisco, CA 94104-4594

Order Form can also be faxed to: **888-481-2665**

PROMO JBNND

Great Resources for Higher Education Professionals

Student Affairs Today

12 issues for $225 (print) / $180 (e)

Get innovative best practices for student affairs plus lawsuit summaries to keep your institution out of legal trouble. It's packed with advice on offering effective services, assessing and funding programs, and meeting legal requirements.

studentaffairstodaynewsletter.com

Campus Legal Advisor

12 issues for $210 (print) / $170 (e)

From complying with the ADA and keeping residence halls safe to protecting the privacy of student information, this monthly publication delivers proven strategies to address the tough legal issues you face on campus.

campuslegaladvisor.com

Campus Security Report

12 issues for $210 (print) / $170 (e)

A publication that helps you effectively manage the challenges in keeping your campus, students, and employees safe. From protecting students on campus after dark to interpreting the latest laws and regulations, *Campus Security Report* has answers you need.

campussecurityreport.com

National Teaching & Learning Forum

6 issues for $65 (print or e)

From big concepts to practical details and from cutting-edge techniques to established wisdom, NTLF is your resource for cross-disciplinary discourse on student learning. With it, you'll gain insights into learning theory, classroom management, lesson planning, scholarly publishing, team teaching, online learning, pedagogical innovation, technology, and more.

ntlf.com

Disability Compliance for Higher Education

12 issues for $230 (print) / $185 (e)

This publication combines interpretation of disability laws with practical implementation strategies to help you accommodate students and staff with disabilities. It offers data collection strategies, intervention models for difficult students, service review techniques, and more.

disabilitycomplianceforhighereducation.com

Dean & Provost

12 issues for $225 (print) / $180 (e)

From budgeting to faculty tenure and from distance learning to labor relations, *Dean & Provost* gives you innovative ways to manage the challenges of leading your institution. Learn how to best use limited resources, safeguard your institution from frivolous lawsuits, and more.

deanandprovost.com

Enrollment Management Report

12 issues for $230 (print) / $185 (e)

Find out which enrollment strategies are working for your colleagues, which aren't, and why. This publication gives you practical guidance on all aspects—including records, registration, recruitment, orientation, admissions, retention, and more.

enrollmentmanagementreport.com

WANT TO SUBSCRIBE?
Go online or call: 888.378.2537.

JB JOSSEY-BASS
A Wiley Brand

Great Resources for Higher Education Professionals

College Athletics and the Law

12 issues for $225 (print) / $180 (e)

Develop a legally sound "game plan" for your institution's athletic programs! Each month, you get expert coaching on how to meet NCAA and Title IX requirements, negotiate coaching contracts, support athletes with disabilities, and more.

collegeathleticslaw.com

FERPA Answer Book and Bulletin

6 issues for $220 (print only)

Includes a full binder with all you need to know about FERPA

From safekeeping students' education records to learning how you can share personal information, this is your professional survival guide. It includes the latest changes to the regs, how to comply, and newly issued FPCO policy letters, administrative and judicial decisions, and more.

About Campus

6 issues for $65 (print only)

An exciting and eclectic mix of articles — designed to illuminate the critical issues faced by both student affairs and academic affairs as they work on their shared goal: to help students learn. Topics include promoting student learning, meeting the needs of a diverse student population, assessing student learning, and accommodating the changing student culture.

Assessment Update

6 issues for $135 (print) / $110 (e)

Get the latest assessment techniques for higher education. *Assessment Update* is your resource for evaluating learning communities, performance indicators, assessing student engagement, using electronic portfolios, new assessment approaches and more.

assessmentupdate.com

Recruiting & Retaining Adult Learners

12 issues for $225 (print) / $180 (e)

This publication addresses the challenges and opportunities you face in recruiting, retaining, and educating your adult students. Find strategies to target your orientation to adult learners, encourage adult-friendly support systems, take advantage of new technologies, and more.

recruitingretainingadultlearners.com

The Successful Registrar

12 issues for $230 (print) / $185 (e)

Get practical guidance on all aspects of your job—from implementing the newest technology and successful registration programs to complying with FERPA, and from training your staff and student workers to security issues and transcript management.

thesuccessfulregistrar.com

The Department Chair

4 issues for $99 (print) / $89 (e)

From retaining your best faculty and resolving conflict to measuring learning and implementing new policies, this resource arms you with the practical information you need to manage your department effectively.

departmentchairs.org/journal.aspx

WANT TO SUBSCRIBE?

Go online or call: 888.378.2537.

JB JOSSEY-BASS
A Wiley Brand